Microsoft® Office Access® 2010

Level 1 (Second Edition)

Microsoft® Office Access® 2010: Level 1 (Second Edition)

Part Number: 084306
Course Edition: 1.0

NOTICES

What is the Microsoft Office Specialist Certification Program?

The Microsoft Office Specialist (MOS) Certification Program enables candidates to show that they have something exceptional to offer - proven expertise in Microsoft® Office applications. The MOS Certification Program is the only Microsoft-approved certification program of its kind. The MOS Certification exams focus on validating specific skill sets within each of the Microsoft® Office system programs. The candidate can choose which exam(s) they want to take according to which skills they want to validate. The available MOS exams include:

- MOS: Microsoft® Office Word 2010
- MOS: Microsoft® Office Excel® 2010
- MOS: Microsoft® Office PowerPoint® 2010
- MOS: Microsoft® Office Outlook® 2010
- MOS: Microsoft® Office Access® 2010
- MOS: Microsoft® SharePoint® 2010

For more information:

HELP US IMPROVE OUR COURSEWARE

Your comments are important to us. Please contact us at Element K Press LLC, 1-800-478-7788, 500 Canal View Boulevard, Rochester, NY 14623, Attention: Product Planning, or through our Web site at **http://support.elementkcourseware.com**.

To learn more about MOS exams, visit **www.microsoft.com/learning/en/us/certification/mos.aspx**.

Microsoft® Office Access® 2010: Level 1 (Second Edition)

Lesson 6: Generating Reports

Appendix A: Microsoft Office Access 2010 Exam 77–885

About This Course

Most organizations maintain and manage large amounts of information. One of the most efficient and powerful ways of managing data is by using relational databases. Information can be stored, linked, and managed by using a single relational database application and its associated tools. In this course, you will examine the basic database concepts and create and modify databases and their various objects by using the Microsoft® Office Access® 2010 relational database application.

Managing large amounts of complex information is common in today's business environment and, if done properly, can provide any business an edge over the competition. However, mismanaged and lost information can cause you to fall behind. Managing data by using the Access 2010 database application can give your business that positive edge.

This course can also benefit you if you are preparing to take the Microsoft Office Specialist (MOS) Certification exams for Microsoft® Access® 2010. Please refer to the CD-ROM that came with this course for document that map exam objectives to the content in the Microsoft Office Access courseware series. To access the mapping document, insert the CD-ROM into your CD-ROM drive and at the root of the CD, double-click ExamMapping.doc to open the mapping document. In addition to the mapping document, two assessment files per course can be found on the CD-ROM to check your knowledge. To access the assessments, at the root of the course part number folder, double-click 084306s3.doc to view the assessments without the answers marked, or double-click 084306ie.doc to view the assessments with the answers marked.

If your course manual did not come with a CD-ROM, please go to **http://www.elementk.com/courseware-file-downloads** to download the files.

Course Description

Target Student

This course is designed for students who wish to learn the basic operations of the Microsoft Access database program to perform their day-to-day responsibilities, and who want to use the application to be more productive in their work. It provides the fundamental knowledge and techniques needed to use more complex Access features such as maintaining databases and using programming techniques that enhance Access applications.

Course Prerequisites

You should be familiar with using personal computers. You should be comfortable in the Windows environment and be able to use Windows to manage information on the computer. Specifically, you should be able to launch and close programs; navigate to information stored on the computer; and manage files and folders. To ensure your success, we recommend that you first take one of Element K's introductory Windows courses, such as either of the following, or have equivalent skills and knowledge:

- *Windows XP Professional: Level 1*
- *Windows XP: Introduction*

Course Objectives

In this course, you will create and modify new databases and their various objects.

You will:

- Identify the basic components of an Access database.
- Build the structure of a database.
- Manage data in tables.
- Query a database.
- Design forms.
- Generate reports.

Certification

This course is designed to help you prepare for the following certification.

Certification Path: MOS: Microsoft Office Access 2010 Exam 77–885

This course is one of a series of Element K courseware titles that addresses Microsoft Office Specialist (MOS) certification skill sets. The MOS and certification program is for individuals who use Microsoft's business desktop software and who seek recognition for their expertise with specific Microsoft products.

How to Use This Book

As a Learning Guide

This book is divided into lessons and topics, covering a subject or a set of related subjects. In most cases, lessons are arranged in order of increasing proficiency.

The results-oriented topics include relevant and supporting information you need to master the content. Each topic has various types of activities designed to enable you to practice the guidelines and procedures as well as to solidify your understanding of the informational material presented in the course.

At the back of the book, you will find a glossary of the definitions of the terms and concepts used throughout the course. You will also find an index to assist in locating information within the instructional components of the book.

In the Classroom

This book is intended to enhance and support the in-class experience. Procedures and guidelines are presented in a concise fashion along with activities and discussions. Information is provided for reference and reflection in such a way as to facilitate understanding and practice.

Each lesson may also include a Lesson Lab or various types of simulated activities. You will find the files for the simulated activities along with the other course files on the enclosed CD-ROM. If your course manual did not come with a CD-ROM, please go to **http://www.elementk.com/courseware-file-downloads** to download the files. If included, these interactive activities enable you to practice your skills in an immersive business environment, or to use hardware and software resources not available in the classroom. The course files that are available on the CD-ROM or by download may also contain sample files, support files, and additional reference materials for use both during and after the course.

As a Teaching Guide

Effective presentation of the information and skills contained in this book requires adequate preparation. As such, as an instructor, you should familiarize yourself with the content of the entire course, including its organization and approaches. You should review each of the student activities and exercises so you can facilitate them in the classroom.

Throughout the book, you may see Instructor Notes that provide suggestions, answers to problems, and supplemental information for you, the instructor. You may also see references to "Additional Instructor Notes" that contain expanded instructional information; these notes appear in a separate section at the back of the book. PowerPoint slides may be provided on the included course files, which are available on the enclosed CD-ROM or by download from **http://www.elementk.com/courseware-file-downloads** The slides are also referred to in the text. If you plan to use the slides, it is recommended to display them during the corresponding content as indicated in the Instructor Notes in the margin.

The course files may also include assessments for the course, which can be administered diagnostically before the class, or as a review after the course is completed. These exam-type questions can be used to gauge the students' understanding and assimilation of course content.

As a Review Tool

Any method of instruction is only as effective as the time and effort you, the student, are willing to invest in it. In addition, some of the information that you learn in class may not be important to you immediately, but it may become important later. For this reason, we encourage you to spend some time reviewing the content of the course after your time in the classroom.

As a Reference

The organization and layout of this book make it an easy-to-use resource for future reference. Taking advantage of the glossary, index, and table of contents, you can use this book as a first source of definitions, background information, and summaries.

Course Icons

Icon	Description
	A **Caution Note** makes students aware of potential negative consequences of an action, setting, or decision that are not easily known.
	Display Slide provides a prompt to the instructor to display a specific slide. Display Slides are included in the Instructor Guide only.
	An **Instructor Note** is a comment to the instructor regarding delivery, classroom strategy, classroom tools, exceptions, and other special considerations. Instructor Notes are included in the Instructor Guide only.
	Notes Page indicates a page that has been left intentionally blank for students to write on.
	A **Student Note** provides additional information, guidance, or hints about a topic or task.
	A **Version Note** indicates information necessary for a specific version of software.

Course Requirements

Hardware

For this course, you will need one computer for each student and one for the instructor. Each computer will need the following minimum hardware components:

- 1 GHz Pentium-class processor or faster
- Minimum 256 MB of RAM. 1 GB of RAM is recommended
- 20 GB of hard disk space or larger. You should have at least 1 GB of free hard disk space available for the Office installation.
- A DVD-ROM drive
- A keyboard and mouse or other pointing device.
- 1024 x 768 resolution monitor recommended
- Network cards and cabling for local network access
- Internet access (contact your local network administrator)
- Printer (optional) or an installed printer driver (Printers are not required; however, each PC must have an installed printer driver to use Print Preview.)
- Projection system to display the instructor's computer screen

Software

- Microsoft® Office Professional Plus 2010 Edition
- Microsoft® Windows® XP Professional with Service Pack 3

This course was developed using the Windows XP operating system. If you use Windows Vista or Windows 7, you might notice some slight differences when keying in the course.

Class Setup

Initial Class Setup

For initial class setup:

1. Install Windows XP Professional on an empty partition.

    ■ Leave the Administrator password blank.

    ■ For all other installation parameters, use values that are appropriate for your environment (see your local network administrator for details).

2. On Windows XP Professional, disable the **Welcome** screen. (This step ensures that students will be able to log on as the Administrator user regardless of what other user accounts exist on the computer.)

    a. Click **Start** and choose **Control Panel→User Accounts.**

    b. Click **Change The Way Users Log On And Off.**

    c. Uncheck **Use Welcome Screen.**

    d. Click **Apply Options.**

3. On Windows XP Professional, install Service Pack 3. Use the Service Pack installation defaults.

4. On the computer, install a printer driver (a physical print device is optional). Click **Start** and choose **Printers and Faxes.** Under **Printer Tasks,** click **Add a Printer** and follow the prompts.

    If you do not have a physical printer installed, right-click the printer and choose **Pause Printing** to prevent any print error message.

5. Run the **Internet Connection Wizard** to set up the Internet connection as appropriate for your environment, if you did not do so during installation.

6. Display the known file type extensions.

    a. Right-click **Start** and then select **Explore** to open Windows Explorer.

    b. Choose **Tools→Folder Options.**

    c. On the **View** tab, in the **Advanced Settings** list box, uncheck **Hide Extensions For Known File Types.**

    d. Click **Apply** and then click **OK.**

    e. Close Windows Explorer.

7. Log on to the computer as the Administrator user if you have not already done so.

8. Perform a complete installation of Microsoft Office Professional Plus 2010.

9. In the **User Name** dialog box, click **OK** to accept the default user name and initials.

10. In the **Microsoft Office 2010 Activation Wizard** dialog box, click **Next** to activate the Office 2010 application.

11. When the activation of Microsoft Office 2010 is complete, click **Close** to close the **Microsoft Office 2010 Activation Wizard** dialog box.

12. In the **User Name** dialog box, click **OK.**

13. In the **Welcome To Microsoft 2010** dialog box, click **Finish.** You must have an active Internet connection to complete this step. Select the **Download and Install Updates From Microsoft Update When Available (Recommended)** option so that whenever there is a new update it gets automatically installed on your system.

14. After the Microsoft Update runs, in the **Microsoft Office** dialog box, click **OK.**

15. If necessary, minimize the **Language** bar.

16. On the course CD-ROM, open the 084306 folder. Then, open the Data folder. Run the 084306dd.exe self-extracting file located within. This will install a folder named 084306Data on your C drive. This folder contains all the data files that you will use to complete this course. If your course did not come with a CD, please go to **http:// elementkcourseware.com** to download the data files.

Within each lesson folder, you may find a Solution folder. This folder contains solution files for the lesson's activities and lesson lab, which can be used by students to check their end results.

Customize the Windows Desktop

Customize the Windows desktop to display the **My Computer** and **My Network Places** icons:

1. On the desktop, right-click and choose **Properties.**

2. Select the **Desktop** tab.

3. Click **Customize Desktop.**

4. In the **Desktop Items** dialog box, check **My Computer** and **My Network Places.**

5. Click **OK** and click **Apply.**

6. Close the **Display Properties** dialog box.

Configure Trust Center Settings

To configure **Trust Center** settings:

1. On the **File** tab, choose **Options** to display the **Access Options** dialog box.

2. In the left pane, select **Trust Center.**

3. In the right pane, in the **Microsoft Access Trust Center** section, click **Trust Center Settings.**

4. In the **Trust Center** dialog box, select **Macro Settings,** select the **Enable All Macros** option, and click **OK.**

5. Select the **Trusted Locations** option and click **Add new location.**

6. In the **Microsoft Office Trusted Location** dialog box, click the **Browse** button, navigate to the C:\084306Data folder, and click **OK.**

7. Check **Subfolders of this location are also trusted.**

8. In the **Microsoft Office Trusted Location** dialog box, click **OK.**

9. Click **OK** to close the **Trust Center** dialog box.

10. Click **OK** to close the **Access Options** dialog box.

Before Every Class

1. Log on to the computer as the Administrator user.

2. Delete any existing data file from the C:\084306Data folder.

3. Extract a fresh copy of the course data files from the CD-ROM provided with the course manual, or download the data files from **http://elementkcourseware.com**.

4. Back up the C:\084306Data folder. Overwrite the C:\084306Data folder with the backed up folder if you want to perform the activities again.

List of Additional Files

Printed with each activity is a list of files students open to complete that activity. Many activities also require additional files that students do not open, but are needed to support the file(s) students are working with. These supporting files are included with the student data files on the course CD-ROM or data disk. Do not delete these files.

1 Getting Started with Access Databases

Lesson Time: 45 minutes

Lesson Objectives:

In this lesson, you will identify the basic components of an Access database.

You will:

- Identify the elements of the Access 2010 interface.
- Identify the components of a database.
- Examine the process of creating a relational database.

Introduction

In most businesses, there are those whose jobs depend on working with large amounts of varying types of data. Before creating your first database to manage large volumes of data, it is important that you get familiar with an application that allows you to create and use databases and consider the key aspects of good database design. In this lesson, you will get started with databases in Access 2010.

Learning something new starts with learning to perform the most basic set of tasks, and this holds true for learning how to work with a new application also. By identifying the components of the Access 2010 interface, and gaining an understanding of database attributes and database design, you can begin to plan, design, create, and manage robust databases.

TOPIC A

Identify the Elements of the Access 2010 Interface

You are required to use Access 2010 to manage data in your organization. To work effectively with the application, you need to familiarize yourself with the interface layout and the commands, options, and tools available. In this topic, you will identify the elements of the Access 2010 user interface.

While working on a new software application, you could potentially waste a significant amount of time searching for specific options in the work environment. You can prevent this by familiarizing yourself with the user interface elements. Having this basic level of competence is the first step toward achieving the output that you are seeking when you begin using the application for business requirements.

Microsoft Access 2010

Microsoft Access 2010 is a database application that is part of the Microsoft Office 2010 suite. Its user-friendly interface components help you create databases and keep data updated for quick retrieval. Access 2010 provides you with various features to input, store, and output data, and allows you to import and export data from and to external applications. You can also easily access help resources, which provide information on both database concepts and Access tasks.

The Access 2010 Application Window

The Access 2010 application window displays components that are designed to help you create, enhance, and manage databases in Access.

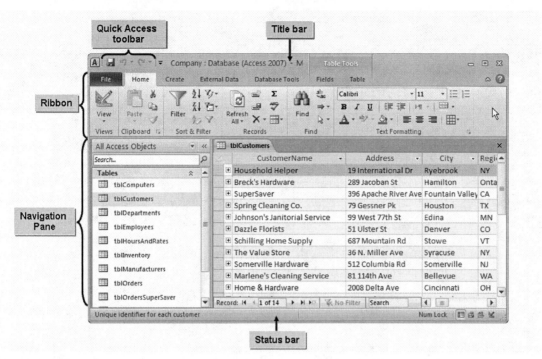

Figure 1-1: *The components of the Microsoft Access 2010 window.*

Component	Description
The title bar	A bar at the top of the application window that displays the name of the open database.
The Ribbon	A panel at the top of the application window that contains application commands. These commands are organized into tabs and groups.
The Quick Access toolbar	A toolbar at the top-left corner of the application window that contains frequently used commands such as **Save, Undo,** and **Redo.** This toolbar can also be positioned below the Ribbon, and can be customized to include additional commands.
The Navigation Pane	A pane at the left side of the application window that displays database objects such as tables, queries, forms, and reports. You can also minimize the Navigation Pane and customize its display.
The status bar	A bar at the bottom of the application window that displays the current application status, along with the viewing options for the current database object. It also displays information about the current database object and the status of keys such as **Caps Lock, Scroll Lock,** and **Num Lock.** Information on the status bar can be displayed or hidden.

Tabbed Document Windows

Access displays open database objects, such as tables, queries, and forms, as tabs in the same window. Each tab represents one of the open database objects, making it convenient to switch to working on any object by selecting its tab.

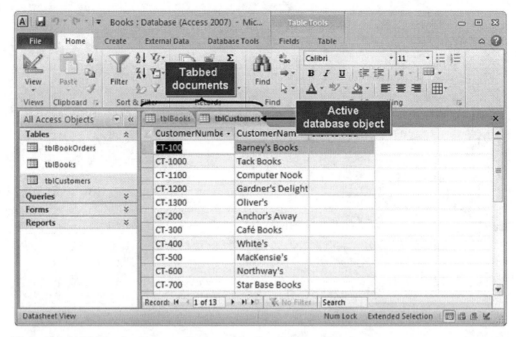

Figure 1-2: *Tabbed windows displayed in the Access interface.*

The Ribbon

The *Ribbon* is a panel at the top of the application window that contains easy-to-browse commands, which you can use to work on a database. The tabs are organized in the order in which they will be used in the process of creating a database. Each tab is divided into groups of commands that allow you to perform specific tasks. The Ribbon can also be customized by adding or removing tabs, groups, and individual commands that are present in each group. You can hide the Ribbon by double-clicking any active tab or by clicking the **Minimize the Ribbon** button.

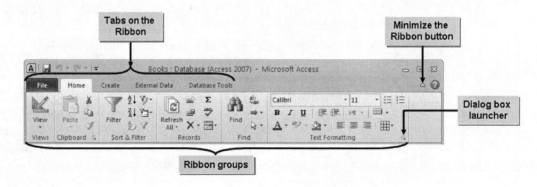

Figure 1-3: *The Ribbon with its default tabs.*

ScreenTips

A *ScreenTip* is a short descriptive piece of text that is displayed when you hover the mouse pointer over a command on the Ribbon. It displays the name of the command, and may include a description and shortcut to access the command.

Dialog Box Launchers

Dialog box launchers are small buttons with a downward pointing arrow located at the bottom-right corner of certain groups on the Ribbon. You can use them to launch dialog boxes or task panes that contain commands that are specific to the features found in that group. These dialog boxes and panes are used to adjust the settings that are not accessible from the Ribbon.

The Ribbon Tabs

The Ribbon tabs allow you to access commands that perform simple or advanced operations without having to navigate extensively.

Ribbon Tab	Contains
File	Commands for opening, saving, and closing a database. It also displays an interface called the Backstage view with commands to perform additional tasks such as to restrict access to the database and help prevent database problems and repair them.
Home	The most commonly used commands that enable you to start working with a database. It contains functional groups for viewing, organizing, and manipulating data present in the database objects and for formatting data.
Create	Groups with commands for the creation of database objects such as tables, forms, queries, and reports.
External Data	Groups with commands to import data from and export data to other applications.
Database Tools	Groups for manipulating macros, defining relationships, showing or hiding specific tools, analyzing data, moving data to a server, and accessing database tools.

The Backstage View

The *Backstage view* in Access 2010 is an interface that is displayed when you select the **File** tab. It contains a series of tabs that group similar commands. It simplifies access to the application-oriented features in Access and lets you save, print, and share databases with a few mouse clicks.

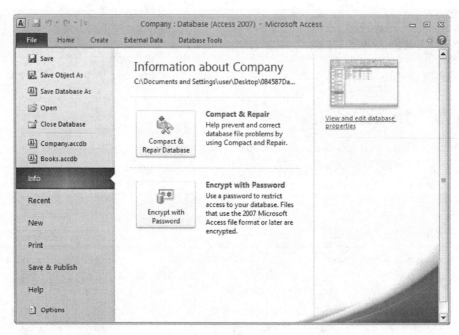

Figure 1-4: *The Backstage view displaying options on the File tab.*

The commands in the Backstage view allow you to perform a wide variety of functions.

File Tab Command	Allows You To
Save	Save changes to a database or database object.
Save Object As	Save an existing object as a different database object or with a different name or publish the object as a PDF file.
Save Database As	Save an existing database with a new file name and in a new location.
Open	Open an existing database.
Close Database	Close an open database.
Info	Share a database with others. It provides access to relationship tools that help define data relationships in tables. It also provides options to correct and fix database issues, view object dependencies, analyze the performance of a database, restrict access to other users, and view and edit database properties.
Recent	View the recently accessed databases and open them. You can also pin or clear pinned databases by using the right-click context menu.
New	Create a blank database or a blank web database, access the recent templates used, and choose from the predefined templates or custom designed templates, or create a new template from an existing one. You can also access community templates, which are published by other Access users.
Print	Preview and print an object after selecting a printer and specifying printer settings.

File Tab Command	Allows You To
Save & Publish	Save the open database file. It also provides options to save a database in the format of the previous Access version, save it as a database template, package a database, apply a digital signature, back up a database, save a database to a document management server, and publish the database to be shared through web browsers and SharePoint.
Help	View online and internal help options and access the **Access Options** dialog box.
Options	Customize Access by using the **Access Options** dialog box.
Exit	Exit the application.

Contextual Information

The Backstage view also displays certain information on a contextual basis; that is the information is displayed on the occurrence of a certain event. For example, if the database you are working on has some active content that is disabled, the **Security Warning** section in the Backstage view displays additional information that will enable you to fix that issue.

Contextual Tabs

Contextual tabs are additional tabs displayed on the Ribbon when you work with objects such as tables, forms, queries, or reports. The commands and options available on these tabs are restricted to only those that can be used to manipulate the objects the tab appears for. These tabs are displayed along with the core tabs of the Ribbon and can be used to modify and format the objects that are displayed. You can switch between the contextual tabs and the core tabs as needed.

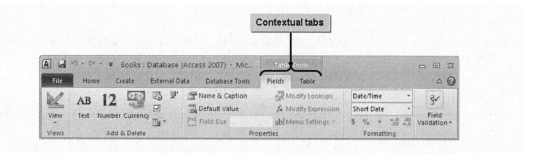

Figure 1-5: The commands on the Fields contextual tab on the Table Tools tool tab.

Access Help

The *Access Help feature* is a repository of information about the functionality of Microsoft Access 2010 features. Access Help provides answers to Access-related queries. Some of the help information is located on the computer's hard drive; some drawn from the web. You can also search for information by browsing through the links that are already provided or by performing keyword-based searches.

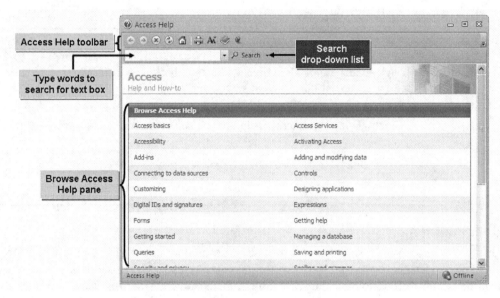

Figure 1-6: *Components of the Access Help window.*

The *Access Help window* contains a number of components that will help you find answers to Access-related queries.

Component	Description
The **Access Help** toolbar	Provides access to navigate, print, and format help content.
The **Type words to search for** text box and drop-down list	Allows you to type the keyword about which you need to search for information. Previously used keywords can be found in the **Type words to search for** drop-down list.
The **Search** drop-down list	Provides options to search for information from online or offline content.
The **Browse Access Help** pane	Displays the topics available in Access Help. You can navigate to a topic by clicking it.

The Access Help Toolbar

The *Access Help toolbar* provides buttons that enable you to quickly navigate through the Help system.

Button	Allows You To
Back	Navigate to the page that was previously accessed.
Forward	Navigate to the next page. The **Forward** button is enabled only after the **Back** button has been used.
Stop	Stop the search that is in progress.
Refresh	Refresh the page that is displayed.
Home	Display the **Home** page of Access Help.
Print	Print a **Help** page with specific options.

Button	Allows You To
Change Font Size	Increase or decrease the font size of the text in a Help topic.
Show Table of Contents	Display the task pane, which contains the table of contents of Access Help.
Keep On Top/Not On Top	Set the Help window to stay on top of other Access windows or display other Access windows on top of the Help window. By clicking the **Keep On Top** button, you can toggle to the **Not On Top** button.

Areas of Search in Access Help

You can use the Access Help feature available within the application, or select an option from the **Content From Office Online** section to search the web for help on the desired topic. You can use the **Search Access Help** drop-down list to narrow the search results to a specific area.

Area of Search	Lists
All Access	Information on the query from the built-in Help feature and provides help links to resources in the Microsoft Office website, if required.
Access Help	Information on the query from the built-in Help feature as well as the Microsoft Office website, but does not link you to the Office website.
Access Templates	Sample templates that are available in the Microsoft Office website.
Access Training	Sample training information links to resources in the Microsoft Office website.
Developer Reference	Programming tasks, samples, and references to guide you in developing customized solutions based on Access.

ACTIVITY 1-1

Exploring the Access User Interface

Data Files:

C:\084306Data\Getting Started with Access Databases\Books.accdb

Scenario:

Our Global Company (OGC) is a conglomerate that offers a wide variety of products and services with branches throughout the world. The retail division of the company is OGC Retail. You are a new recruit in the finance department of OGC Retail. One of your tasks includes creating and updating databases for your department using Access 2010, which you are not familiar with. You decide to spend some time familiarizing yourself with the Access 2010 interface.

1. Open an existing database.

   a. Choose **Start→All Programs→Microsoft Office→Microsoft Access 2010** to launch the application.

   b. On the **File** tab, choose **Open.**

    Ensure that you configure the trust center settings given under the heading **Configure Trust Center Settings** to enable smooth working of Access database.

   c. In the **Open** dialog box, navigate to the C:\084306Data\Getting Started with Access Databases folder.

   d. Select **Books.accdb** and click **Open.**

   e. In the Navigation Pane, in the **Tables** section, double-click **tblBookOrders** to open the table.

   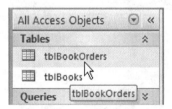

2. Explore the Quick Access toolbar.

a.   On the Quick Access toolbar, place the mouse pointer over the **Save** button to view its ScreenTip.

b.   On the Quick Access toolbar, click the **Customize Quick Access Toolbar** drop-down arrow, ▾ to view the **Customize Quick Access Toolbar** menu.

c.   On the **Customize Quick Access Toolbar** menu, observe that the **Save, Undo,** and **Redo** commands are checked, indicating that these commands are displayed on the Quick Access toolbar.

d.   Click the **Customize Quick Access Toolbar** drop-down arrow again to close the **Customize Quick Access Toolbar** menu.

3.   Explore the Ribbon.

a.   On the **Home** tab, observe the **Views, Clipboard, Sort & Filter, Records, Find,** and **Text Formatting** groups.

b.   On the Ribbon, select the **Create** tab.

c.   Observe the commands on the **Create** tab.

d.   On the Ribbon, at the right corner of the Access window, place the mouse pointer over the **Minimize the Ribbon** button, ⌃ to view its ScreenTip.

e.   On the Ribbon, click the **Minimize the Ribbon** button to collapse the Ribbon.

f.   On the Ribbon, click the **Expand the Ribbon** button to expand the Ribbon.

4.   Explore the Backstage view.

a.   Select the **File** tab.

b. Observe that the Backstage view is displayed with the options to save, open, and close.

c. On the **File** tab, choose **New,** and in the **Available Templates** pane, select **Sample templates** to display a thumbnail view of the sample templates.

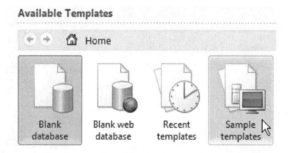

d. Click the **Back** button,  to navigate to the previous page, and in the **Office.com Templates** section, select **Assets.**

e. In the **Available Templates** pane, in the **Office.com Templates** section, observe the templates that are available for downloading from the Office.com website.

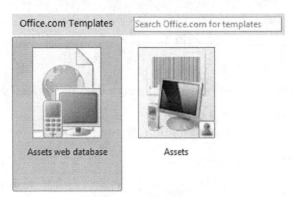

5. Display the **Datasheet Formatting** dialog box using a dialog box launcher.

a. On the Ribbon, select the **Home** tab.

b. In the **Text Formatting** group, at the bottom-right corner, click the **Datasheet For-matting** dialog box launcher.

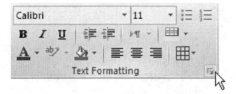

c. Observe that the **Datasheet Formatting** dialog box is displayed.

d. In the **Datasheet Formatting** dialog box, click the **Close** button to close the dialog box.

6. View the content of a Help topic.

a. At the top-right corner of the Ribbon, click the **Microsoft Access Help** button.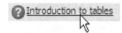

b. At the top-right corner of the Access Help window, click the **Maximize** button to maximize the Access Help window.

c. On the Access Help toolbar, click the **Show Table of Contents** button.

d. In the **Table of Contents** pane, observe the various help topics that are displayed and click the **Access basics** link.

e. In the **Access basics** section, click the **Introduction to tables** link.

f. In the right pane, scroll down to view an overview of tables.

7. Search for information about the Ribbon.

a. At the top-left corner of the Access Help window, in the **Type words to search for** text box, click and type ***ribbon***

b. Click **Search.**

c. Observe that in the **Access** pane, links to information about the Ribbon are displayed.

d. In the **Access** pane, click the **Customize the Ribbon** link to view its content.

e. In the **Table of Contents** pane, observe that the contents change according to the selected topic.

f. At the top-right corner of the Access Help window, click the **Close** button to close the Access Help window.

g. At the top-right corner of the document window, click the **Close** button, ☒ to close the tblBookOrders table.

> Do not click the **Close** button at the top-right corner of the application window, as this would close Microsoft Access.

TOPIC B

Identify the Components of a Database

You have identified the user interface and tools in Access. Now that you will be using Access, you may want to gain an understanding of databases and the terms used to describe database components as the first step to become a competent database user. In this topic, you will identify the components of a database.

When working with a database application for the first time, you could potentially waste a significant amount of time trying to understand how a database functions. You can prevent this by identifying the components of a database and the functionality provided by each component. Gaining this knowledge will help you achieve the desired result when you begin creating databases.

Databases

Definition:

A *database* is a collection of data that is logically related and organized so that a computer program can access the desired information quickly. A database contains textual, numeric, or graphical data. The data in a database can be searched, retrieved, and manipulated.

Example:

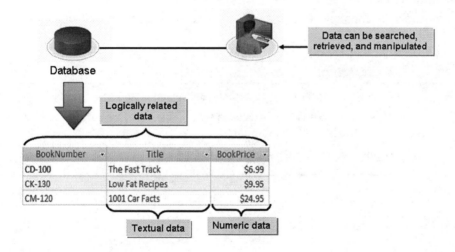

Figure 1-7: A collection of data in a database.

Tables

Definition:

A *table* is a storage container that stores related data in rows and columns. Rows display information about each item in the table. Columns display categories in the table. A table has a header row with a descriptor for each column.

Example:

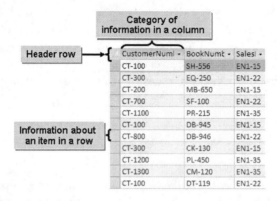

Figure 1-8: A table with information arranged in rows and columns.

Table Components

Tables contain various components that can be individually accessed and manipulated.

Term	Description
Record	A set of data pertaining to a single entity and stored in a row of a table.
Field	A unit of data in a record containing specific information. Fields are represented by the columns of a table.
Value	A single piece of data stored in a field.

Queries

Definition:

A *query* is an instruction that requests data from one or more database tables. In addition to retrieving data, queries can also perform calculations and display the results. Queries can be saved for reuse.

Example:

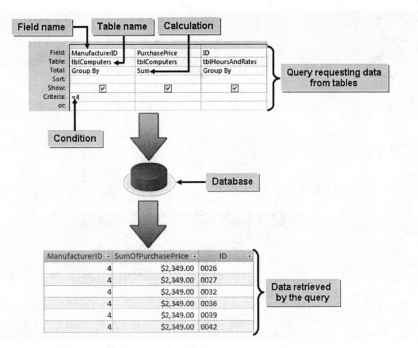

Figure 1-9: A query that retrieves information from specific rows in tables.

Forms

Definition:

A *form* is a graphical interface that is used to add, display, and edit data. Forms can be based on a table or a query, or on multiple tables and queries. Data is never stored in forms; a form only displays the data stored in a table or retrieved by a query. Forms can be customized according to the viewing needs of the user. In addition to displaying table data, forms can include calculated values, graphics, and other objects.

Example:

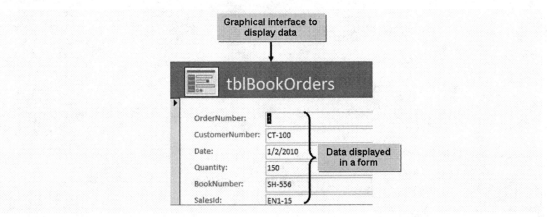

Figure 1-10: A form displaying data from a table.

Reports

Definition:

A *report* is an output of data that is arranged in a format specified by the user. It consists of information retrieved from tables or by queries. Reports can also display the results of calculations performed on data. Reports are often created for the purpose of printing data.

Example:

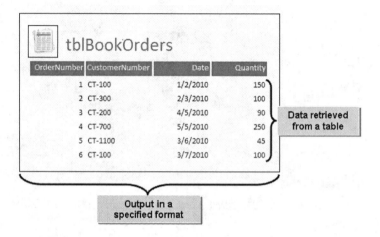

Figure 1-11: *Data arranged in a specified report format.*

ACTIVITY 1-2
Identifying the Components of an Access Database

Before You Begin:

The Books.accdb file is open.

Scenario:

You are asked to retrieve certain data from a database. However, you are still unsure about how to use the various database objects to get your job done. You want to familiarize yourself with the database objects before performing the assigned task.

1. View the data in a table.

    a. In the Navigation Pane, in the **Tables** section, double-click **tblBooks** to open the table.

    b. Observe that the data is stored in the BookNumber, Title, and BookPrice fields.

    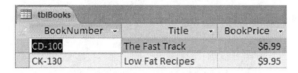

    c. At the top-right corner of the document window, click the **Close** button to close the table.

2. Run a query.

    a. In the Navigation Pane, select **Queries.**

    b. Observe that the list of existing queries in the database is displayed.

    c. Double-click **qryBookOrders** to run the query.

    d. Observe that the customer number, book number, and sales ID details are displayed in the query result.

    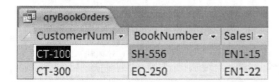

    e. At the top-right corner of the document window, click the **Close** button to close the query.

3. View a form and close it.

    a. In the Navigation Pane, select **Forms.**

    b. Observe that the list of existing forms in the database is displayed.

    c.   Double-click **frmBookOrders** to open the form.

    d.   Observe that the data from a table is displayed in the form.

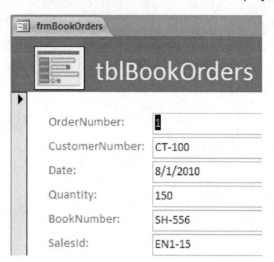

    e.   At the top-right corner of the document window, click the **Close** button to close the form.

4.   View a report and close it.

    a.   In the Navigation Pane, select **Reports.**

    b.   Observe that the list of existing reports in the database is displayed.

    c.   Double-click **rptBooks** to open the report.

    d.   Observe the data that is displayed in the report.

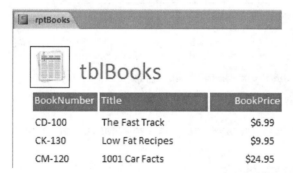

    e.   At the top-right corner of the document window, click the **Close** button to close the report.

    f.   On the Ribbon, select the **File** tab and choose **Close Database.**

TOPIC C

Examine the Relational Database Design Process

You are now familiar with database components. Depending on the data that needs to be stored and retrieved using database components and the purpose of a database, the structure and design of databases will differ. In this topic, you will examine the process of creating a relational database.

With any complicated activity, following a well-defined process will help you stay on track, include all appropriate inputs, and produce the best possible output. Designing a new database is no different. By adhering to the process of designing a relational database, you can ensure that your database will achieve what you aimed for.

Relational Databases

Definition:

Relational databases are databases that store information in multiple tables that are interrelated. Relational databases store information about one entity in each table, and can access these tables to extract, reorganize, and display the information contained within them in many different ways without altering the structure of the original tables.

Example:

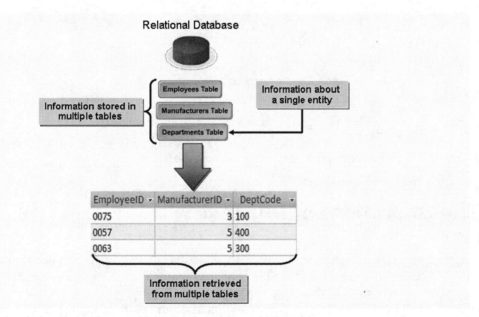

Figure 1-12: A relational database with data stored in multiple tables.

The Relational Database Design Process

The relational database design process consists of seven stages.

1. Identify the purpose of the database.

2. Review the existing data.

3. Make a preliminary list of fields.

4. Organize the fields into tables.

5. Enter sample data, review for possible data maintenance problems, and revise the table design as necessary.

6. Designate primary and foreign keys that can be used to relate your tables together.

7. Determine table relationships.

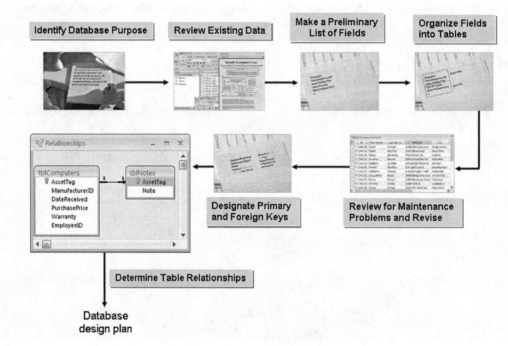

Figure 1-13: *The seven stages of a database design.*

The Statement of Purpose

Definition:

The *statement of purpose* is a clear statement that defines the scope of a database and helps to guide its design. It should imply all kinds of data that will be included in the database, but not state specific table or field names. It can describe the likely types of users of the database, but cannot state specific queries or reports they intend to run. It is sometimes useful to state what the database will not do.

Example:

The database will contain information on:

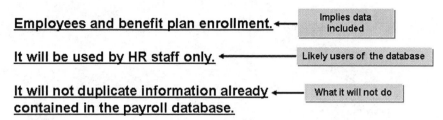

Employees and benefit plan enrollment. ← Implies data included

It will be used by HR staff only. ← Likely users of the database

It will not duplicate information already ← What it will not do
contained in the payroll database.

Figure 1-14: A statement of purpose for a relational database.

Non-Example:

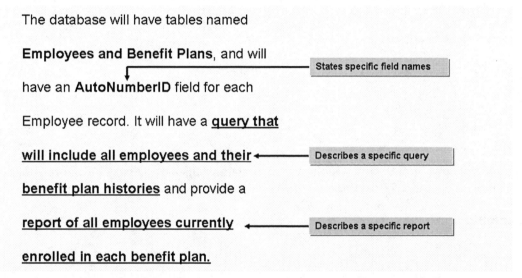

The database will have tables named

Employees and Benefit Plans, and will

have an **AutoNumberID** field for each ← States specific field names

Employee record. It will have a **query that**

will include all employees and their ← Describes a specific query

benefit plan histories and provide a

report of all employees currently ← Describes a specific report

enrolled in each benefit plan.

Figure 1-15: A poorly written statement of purpose.

Existing Data

Definition:

Existing data is information available for you to review as defined in your statement of purpose, and that falls within the scope of your database. It will represent the type of data that is finally stored in your database. This data can be in paper or electronic format. Existing data in a paper format can include internal business forms or documents; third-party or government forms or documents; and printed invoices, bills, or sales slips. Existing data in an electronic format can include spreadsheets, word processing documents, other databases, and web pages.

Example:

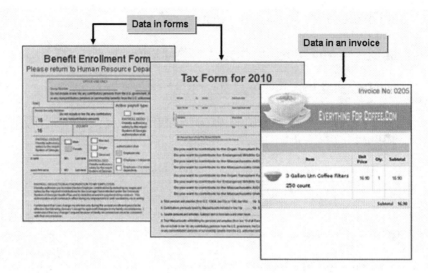

Figure 1-16: Existing data available in forms and invoices.

Fields

Definition:

A *field* is a column of data in a table, which contains a distinct category of information. A field is identified by a unique field name. A table can contain one or more fields.

Example:

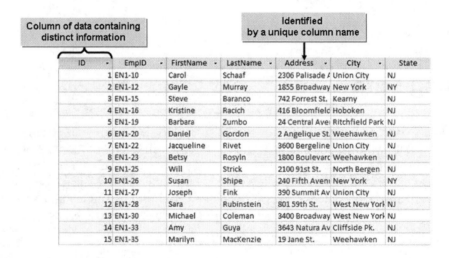

Figure 1-17: A table with fields containing distinct categories of information.

Guidelines to Determine Fields

When you appropriately determine fields, you will meet your users' needs while staying within the scope of your statement of purpose.

Guidelines

To determine fields, be sure to:

- Create a list of fields from existing reports.

    - Determine what parts of the data should be included in the database by examining existing reports.

    - Write a list of calculated fields.

    - Write a list of fields from the existing reports.

- Determine the fields and the calculated fields that are needed based on interviews with potential database users.

    - What data do you expect the database to contain?

    - What kinds of reports would you like to generate from the database?

    - What types of summary information do you expect the database to produce?

    - What kinds of questions do you want the database to be able to answer?

- Complete the list of fields and calculated fields for the database.

 If you are the only potential user of the database you are designing, then you need to consider these questions yourself. It is still an essential stage in the process and should not be skipped.

Example: Determining Fields for a Table

You are designing a database to track the enrollment of employees in benefit plans. You reviewed existing data and now need to determine the fields. You have looked at the application forms that employees use to enroll in benefit plans, and determined that the Employee Code and Plan Enrollment Date are fields that are to be included in your database. When interviewing the other members of the Human Resources department, you begin by making your statement of purpose clear. You then ask them what reports they need to run and what summary information they need to obtain. They indicate that they would like to know the number of employees enrolled in a particular plan and how many have joined each plan during each month. As a result of these interviews, you understand that you need to include Employee Plan and Plan Enroll Date as fields in your table.

Business Rules

Business rules are company procedures and policies that affect the input of data in the database. Business rules are translated into constraints on how data is stored and manipulated. They are enforced through database design techniques. Business rules influence the data you collect and store, and the manner in which you define relationships between tables. Business rules also influence the types of information that the database can provide, and ensure the integrity of data.

An Example of Business Rules

Each employee in your organization will have a unique Employee ID number. Employees can have more than one job function, depending on whether they are scheduled to work as a cashier, a re-stocker, or as a customer service representative at the information desk. Each job function might involve a different hourly pay rate. But employees who are promoted to management have only one job title—manager or assistant manager—and they are paid the same amount, no matter what tasks or job functions they perform during a shift. These business rules influence how the employee tables in the database will be designed, and how they interact.

Guidelines to Group Fields into Tables

Grouping fields into tables ensures that data is well organized and enables you to access database information effectively.

Guidelines

When grouping fields into tables, use these guidelines:

- Store information on only one subject in a table.
- Break tables into multiple, smaller tables as needed.
- Identify tables that correspond to tangible objects, such as people.
- Identify fields of the table as properties of the objects the table represents.

Example: The Customers and Orders Tables

You have ensured that the Customers and Orders tables hold a collection of related information on only one subject. You have identified tables that correspond to tangible objects such as customers and orders with properties such as CustomerName and OrderDate that qualify for fields of the table.

Normalization

Definition:

Normalization is the process of organizing data in a database to produce optimized table structures. It usually involves refining a database by reducing complex data in a table into simple and stable table structures. Normalization ensures data integrity in tables by eliminating two issues: data redundancy and inconsistent dependency between them.

Example:

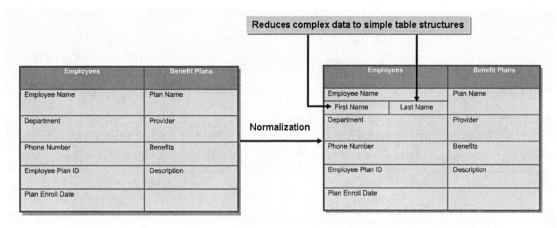

Figure 1-18: *A table and its normalized form.*

Denormalization

Definition:

Denormalization is a database performance optimization process that adds redundant data to tables to speed up database access. During denormalization, data spread across several tables as part of the normalization process might be combined into one table. A database designer may denormalize data to make queries run faster against very large tables, keep similar data together, and keep the overall table structure simple.

Example:

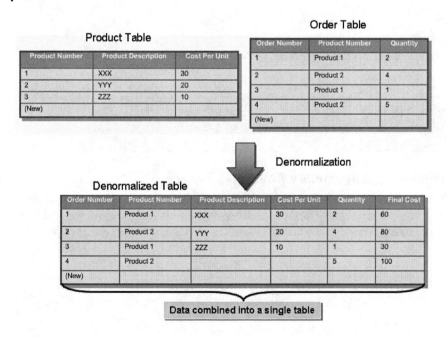

Figure 1-19: *Two tables denormalized to present data in a single table.*

Primary Keys

Definition:

A *primary key* is a field that contains a unique value for each record in a table. The primary key's unique value is used to identify the record. This key establishes a relationship between tables. Primary key fields can be of different data types, but can never be left blank, which means there are never any missing or unknown values. In addition, their values never change.

 The AutoValue property can be set for primary key fields because it guarantees uniqueness.

Example: EmployeeID as a Primary Key

The EmployeeID field is a good candidate for being a primary key for an Employees table.

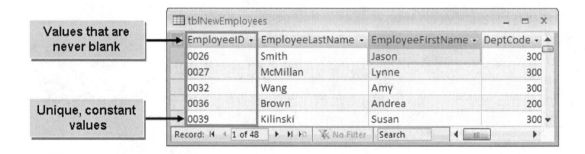

Figure 1-20: A table with a primary key field.

 Other common examples of primary key fields include Student ID, Order Number, Item Code, Part Number, Serial Number, and ISBN Number.

Example: Examples of Bad Primary Keys

A LastName field is not a good primary key field because it can have duplicate values. An Email ID field is not a good primary key field either because it could allow for blank values or because it could change often.

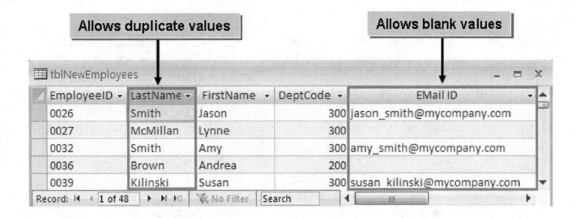

Figure 1-21: *Tables with fields that are not ideal to be designated as primary keys.*

Foreign Keys

Definition:

A *foreign key* is a table field that is linked to the primary key in another table. The two fields must have the same data type. Duplicate values can appear in the foreign key fields. The combination of primary and foreign key fields enables a relational database to store data in multiple tables and retrieve information through queries.

Example: Designate Foreign Keys in Tables

Consider two tables: Employees and Departments. The common field that relates these two tables is DeptCode. Here, the DeptCode field is used as the primary key of the Department table as it is unique and cannot be blank. The values of the DeptCode field of the Employees table tend to repeat for employees working in the same department and therefore will be designated as the foreign key in the Employees table.

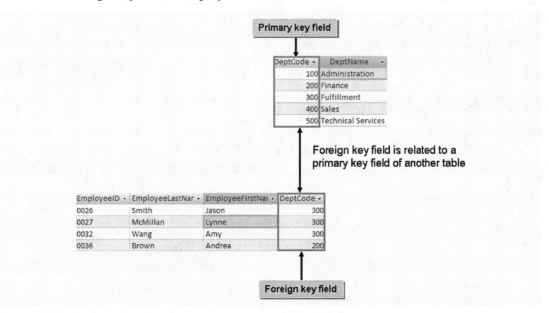

Figure 1-22: *Two tables with primary and foreign key fields.*

Composite Keys

Definition:

A *composite key* is a primary key that uses two or more fields to uniquely identify a record. As in the case of a single field primary key, a composite key will not allow duplicate values.

Example: Designate Composite Keys

Assume that you have three tables: Products, Orders, and Order Details that hold details of various orders undertaken in the company.

1. The Products table consists of information such as ProductID and ProductName.

2. The Orders table consists of primary information such as the OrderID, Date, and CustomerName.

3. The Order Details table consists of information for each product sold, such as OrderID, ProductID, Quantity, UnitPrice, and Discount.

None of the fields in the Order Details table have the capability to uniquely identify a record as all these fields will have repeated values. In such situations, you could choose the OrderID and ProductID fields as a composite key to uniquely identify order details associated with every order.

The Purpose of Primary and Foreign Keys

A primary key acts as an index for all records. It helps establish a relationship between two tables. The foreign key, on the other hand, helps to establish a relationship with a primary key table.

Usage of Primary and Foreign Keys

In a database, the information relating to an entity may be spread across two or more tables. For example, in a bank's database, you can store a customer's details in two different tables: Personal and Transactions. In the Personal table, you will be storing personal information about the customer. In the Transactions table, you will be storing information pertaining to the banking transactions of the customer.

CustomerID values in the Personal table will be unique, and it will be designated as the primary key. The CustomerID values will have multiple occurrences in the Transactions table depending on the number of transactions done by the customer over a period of time.

Table Relationships

Definition:

Table relationships represent the link between data in tables. Defining table relationships helps you pull records from related tables based on matching fields— the primary and foreign keys.

Example:

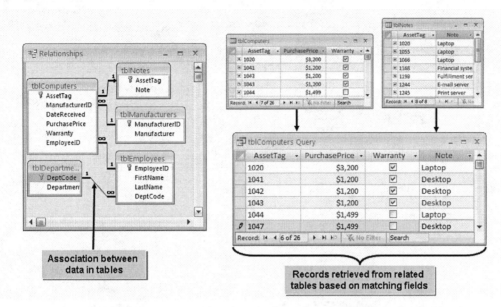

Figure 1-23: A relational database with related tables from which data is retrieved.

Need for Table Relationships

After creating tables in your database and storing information across tables, you need to bring the information back together when needed. This is done by placing common fields in tables that are related and by defining relationships between tables. Defining table relationships helps you create queries, forms, and reports that display information from several tables all at once. They further act as a foundation for ensuring the integrity of the data stored in your database.

One-to-One Relationships

Definition:

A *one-to-one relationship* is a relationship between two tables where both the primary key and the foreign key are unique. For each record in the first table, there will be only one record in the second table. In this relationship, the entity from which a relationship originates is the parent entity and the other is the child entity.

Example:

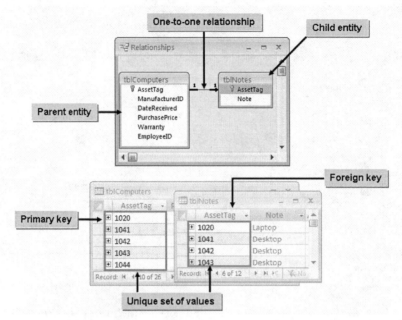

Figure 1-24: *A relationship between two tables where the primary and foreign keys are unique.*

One-to-Many Relationships

Definition:

A *one-to-many relationship* is a relationship between two tables where the primary key is unique, but the foreign key allows duplicate values. For each record in the primary key table, there are multiple records in the foreign key table. A record in the primary key table can also have only one record in the foreign key table.

Example:

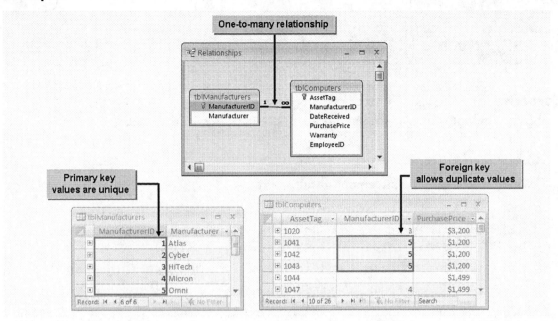

Figure 1-25: *Tables where the primary key is unique, but the foreign key allows duplicate values.*

ACTIVITY 1-3
Analyzing the Relational Database Design Process

Scenario:

In this activity, you will examine the process of designing a relational database.

1. **Which is true about a statement of purpose?**

    a) The statement of purpose should not attempt to list specific table names.

    b) The statement of purpose should not imply the kinds of data that will be included in the database.

    c) The statement of purpose should not describe the likely types of database users.

    d) The statement of purpose should not include a statement of what the database will not do.

2. **In relational database design, what is the task that is performed after the review of existing data is completed?**

    a) Organize fields into tables

    b) Designate primary and foreign keys

    c) Identify the purpose of the database

    d) Make a preliminary list of fields

3. **True or False? Existing data can be available in a paper or an electronic format.**

    __ True

    __ False

4. **Which statement about primary keys is false?**

    a) The primary key field can be left blank.

    b) The primary key is used to identify each record.

    c) The primary key is a field that contains a unique value.

    d) The primary key is used to establish an appropriate relationship between tables.

5. **Which statements about a field are true?**

    a) A field is a column of data.

    b) A field is not known as an attribute.

    c) There can be more than one field in a table.

    d) A field is identified by a unique field name.

Lesson 1 Follow-up

In this lesson, you got acquainted with the Access 2010 environment and basic database concepts. Familiarity with Access and relational database concepts will help you plan, design, create, and maintain robust databases.

1. **Which components in the Access user interface do you find the most useful? Why?**

2. **Which stage in the relational database design process do you think is the most important? Why?**

2 | Building the Structure of a Database

Lesson Time: 1 hour(s), 15 minutes

Lesson Objectives:

In this lesson, you will build the structure of a database.

You will:

- Create a new database.
- Create a table.
- Manage tables in a database.
- Create relationships between tables.

Introduction

You are familiar with Access databases and the guidelines for building one. You may now want to organize data in an Access database. In this lesson, you will build the structure of a database to store data.

A database design is similar to a construction blueprint. Just as constructors need to construct a building frame, you need to build the structure of your database. Building a database from scratch will give you more flexibility. But to create a solid structure, ✦ you should use your design as a strict guide to ensure that you do not deviate from the statement of purpose.

TOPIC A
Create a New Database

You designed a database using the principles of relational database design. The next step is to create a database using Access. In this topic, you will create a new database.

After designing a database, you may find that an existing Access database template offers a structure that is a good fit for your data. In such cases, you may want to create a database using the template to save time. Access has several database templates that you can choose from. However, if your data and workflow do not map to any of the existing database templates, you may have to create a database from scratch. Access also has an option for building a new database.

Database Templates

Access provides predefined templates that can be used as a basis for creating a database. Templates provide the basic structure, layout, formatting, and special characteristics for a database by storing styles and other database elements, such as the default font, page layout settings, and boilerplate text. Each template contains prebuilt tables, forms, queries, and reports that suit the specific purpose of the database.

Community Templates

Access 2010 allows the Access user community to share its databases as templates. You can sign into Office Online by using your Windows Live ID and submit your template by using the **Submit a Template** link on the **Template Submission** page. The submitted template is validated and checked for viruses and then updated to the Templates site from where users can download and access them. Community templates are identified by a pawn icon. Additional information, such as the author name, number of downloads, and star rating, about templates is also displayed in the Backstage view.

Database Saving Options

The **File** tab provides two options to save a database. The **Save Database As** command allows you to save an Access database in a different name in any preferred location. The **Save & Publish** command displays various options in the Backstage view that allow you to save the database in previous versions of Access and also allow you save the database as a template.

How to Create a New Database

Procedure Reference: Create a Blank Database

To create a blank database:

1. On the **File** tab, choose **New.**
2. In the Backstage view, in the **Available Templates** pane, click **Blank Database.**
3. In the right pane, in the **Blank Database** section, in the **File Name** text box, type a name for the database.
4. If necessary, specify the location where you want to store the new database.
   a. Click the **Browse for a location to put your database** button.
   b. In the **File New Database** dialog box, navigate to the desired folder.
   c. Click **OK.**
5. Click **Create** to create a blank database.

Procedure Reference: Create a Template-Based Database

To create a database from a template:

1. On the **File** tab, choose **New.**
2. In the Backstage view, in the **Available Templates** pane, in the **Office.com Templates** section, select the desired category.
3. In the **Office.com Templates** section, select the desired template.
4. In the right pane, in the **File Name** text box, type a name for the database.
5. If necessary, specify the location where you want to store the new database.
6. Click **Download** to open a database based on the template.

Procedure Reference: Save a Database

To save a database:

1. Select the **File** tab.
2. In the Backstage view, specify the save option.
   - Save the database with a different name or in a different location.
     a. Choose **Save Database As.**
     b. In the **Save As** dialog box, navigate to the desired folder.
     c. In the **File name** text box, type the desired file name.
     d. Click **Save.**
   - Save the database in a different version or as a template.
     a. Choose **Save & Publish.**
     b. In the Backstage view, in the **Save Database As** pane, in the **Database File Types** section, select an option.
       - Select **Access Database** to save a copy of the database in the default Access 2010 database format.
       - Select **Access 2002–2003 Database** to save a copy of the database in an Access 2002–2003 compatible format.
       - Select **Access 2000 Database** to save a copy of the database in an Access 2000 compatible format.

- Select **Template** to save the database as a database template.

c. Click **Save As.**

d. In the **Save As** or **Create New Template from This Database** dialog box, specify the desired options and save the database.

ACTIVITY 2-1
Creating a Database

Scenario:
You need to create a database for your organization. You feel that you can start with a table to store the purchase information of computers that are bought every year. Also, you want to create another table to store the contact details of agents who supply hardware equipment to your company.

1. Create a template-based database.

   a. In the Backstage view, in the **Available Templates** pane, observe that the various categories of database templates are listed.

   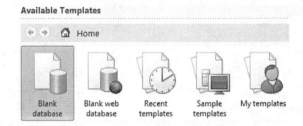

   b. In the **Office.com Templates** section, select **Contacts.**

   c. In the **Available Templates** pane, in the **Office.com Templates** section, select **Contacts web database.**

   d. In the **Contacts web database** pane, in the **File Name** text box, click and type *MyClientContacts*

   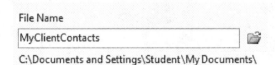

   e. Below the **File Name** text box, observe that the location in which the new file is to be saved is displayed.

   f. To the right of the **File Name** text box, click the **Browse for a location to put your database** button.

   g. In the **File New Database** dialog box, navigate to the C:\084306Data\Building the Structure of a Database folder and click **OK.**

   h. In the Backstage view, in the **Contacts web database** pane, click **Download** to create a database based on the selected template.

   i. Select the **File** tab and choose **Close Database.**

2. Create a blank database.

a.   In the Backstage view, in the **Available Templates** pane, verify that the **Blank database** option is selected.

b.   In the **Blank database** pane, in the **File Name** text box, click and type *MyComputerInventory*

c.   Click the **Browse for a location to put your database** button.

d.   In the **File New Database** dialog box, navigate to the C:\084306Data\Building the Structure of a Database folder and click **OK**.

e.   In the **Blank database** pane, click **Create.**

f.   Observe that a database is created and the name of the database is displayed on the title bar. Also observe that a blank table is displayed.

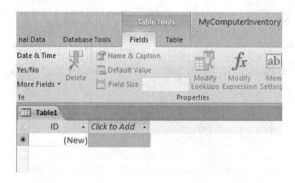

g.   Close the database.

TOPIC B

Create a Table

You created a database. To be able to store data in this database, you need to create tables in it. In this topic, you will create a table to store data.

Once you have defined your table data, you can populate the rows and columns of a table. However, there is more to creating a table than just data entry. You need to know what type of data you are entering, and what view you will use. You also need to know how to modify the rows and columns of the table, and what to do with data that has multiple values. By taking the time to work through these variables, you will be able to create a table that represents information with clarity.

Table Views

You can work with tables in different views, based on the operations to be performed. The most commonly used views are Datasheet and Design views. *Datasheet view* is the default view that displays the data in rows and columns. Each row represents a single record; each column is a field. *Design view* displays all the fields with their data types and descriptions, but does not display the data stored in the table. You can select any field and modify its data type, description, and properties.

Data Types

Each field in a table can be assigned to hold a particular kind of data value called a *data type*.

Data Type	Contains
Text	Alphanumeric characters (text and numbers) as well as symbols and other keyboard characters. This field has a limit of 255 characters.
Memo	Alphanumeric characters and symbols. An improvement on the Text field, this field also supports rich text formatting, and holds up to 2 GB of data.
Number	Numerals only.
Date/Time	Formatted date and time values.
Currency	Number values, formatted with currency symbols such as $ or £. Values are not rounded during calculations and are stored with precision up to four decimal places.
AutoNumber	Unique, sequential numbers created automatically by Access. Typically used as primary keys.
Yes/No	Boolean values. The field can be formatted as True/False, Yes/No, or On/Off.
OLE Object	OLE objects created by another application, such as images, documents, spreadsheets, or charts.
Hyperlink	Email addresses, web site URLS, or network paths.
Attachment	Files created by another application, such as images, documents, spreadsheets, or charts. An improvement on the OLE Object field, this field supports more file types and allows multiple files to be attached to a single record.

Data Type	Contains
Calculated	A calculation using values from other fields in the same table.
Multi-valued	Multiple values. You can create a list of values using the Lookup Wizard.

Field Insertion

You can easily insert a new field in Datasheet or Design view. In Datasheet view, you can add a field by selecting the data type for the field in a new column, and then you can name the field. In the Design view, you can type the name of the field in the **Field Name** column and specify its data type in the **Data Type** column.

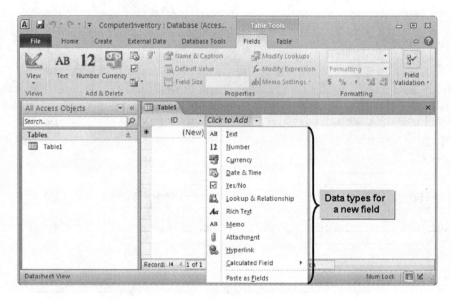

Figure 2-1: *Options to add a field in the Datasheet view.*

Quick Start Fields

You can use Quick Start fields to add multiple fields with a click of the mouse. A variety of pre-formatted fields can be added quickly. This saves time and ensures consistency when creating databases that include tables with similar fields. For example, when you want to add fields for storing addresses, clicking on **Address** in the **Quick Start** section will insert multiple fields such as Address, City, State Province, and more.

You can access the Quick Start fields from the **More Fields** drop-down list in the **Add & Delete** group of the **Table Tools Fields** contextual tab.

Quick Start Field	Adds
Address	The address, city, state province, zip postal, and country region fields in a table.
Category	The category field to a table.
Name	The last name and first name fields to a table.

Quick Start Field	Adds
Payment Type	The payment type field to a table.
Phone	The business phone, home phone, mobile phone, and fax number fields to a table.
Priority	The priority field to a table.
Start and End Dates	The start date and end date fields to a table.
Status	The status field to a table.
Tag	A multi-valued tag field to a table.

The Calendar

When you select a **Date/Time** field, the calendar icon appears to the right of the fields. When you click this icon, a calendar is displayed from which you can select a date. To disable this icon, in Design view, in the **Field Properties** section, set the **Show Date Picker** property to **Never.**

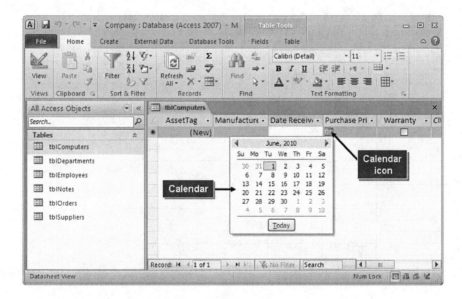

Figure 2-2: *A calendar displayed to enter a value for a date field.*

The Lookup Wizard

The **Lookup Wizard** is used to create a lookup list with values that you can select and enter in a field. You can use the wizard to create two types of lookup lists: value lists and lookup fields. A value list uses a delimited list of items that you enter manually when you use the **Lookup Wizard.** The values in the value lists can be independent of any other data or object in a database. A lookup field uses values from other tables or queries that you can insert in the field. The **Lookup Wizard** can be used to create lookup lists that allow you to enter a value in a field and also to enter values in multi-valued fields.

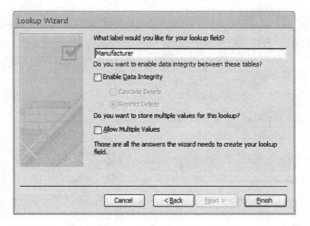

Figure 2-3: The Lookup Wizard displaying options to create a multi-valued field.

How to Create a Table

Procedure Reference: Open a Database

To open a database:

1. Select the **File** tab and choose **Open.**
2. In the **Open** dialog box, navigate to the desired location.
3. Select the desired file and click **Open.**

Procedure Reference: Create a Table

To create a table:

1. On the Ribbon, select the **Create** tab.
2. On the **Create** tab, in the **Tables** group, click **Table.**
3. Insert a field in the table.

   - Insert a field in the table in the Datasheet view.

     a. From the **Click to Add** drop-down list, select a data type.

     b. In the inserted column, replace the default field name with the desired field name.

   - Insert a field in the table in the Design view.

     a. Switch to the Design view.

        - On the **Home** tab, in the **Views** group, click **View** or;
        - On the **Home** tab, in the **Views** group, from the **View** drop-down list, select **Design View** or;
        - On the status bar, click the **Design View** button or;
        - Right-click the table tab and choose **Design View.**

     b. In the document window, in the **Field Name** column, in the desired cell, double-click and type the desired field name.

 If you select **Lookup Wizard** from the drop-down list, you will need to specify the desired settings for creating a multi-valued field.

    c.   In the document window, for the newly inserted field, click in the **Data Type** column, and from the drop-down list, select the desired data type.

4.   If necessary, add more fields to the table.

5.   If necessary, set a field as a primary key.

    a.   Move the mouse pointer before a field until it turns into an arrow and click to select the field.

    b.   On the **Design** contextual tab, in the **Tools** group, click **Primary Key** to set the selected field as the primary key.

6.   Save the table.

    a.   Display the **Save As** dialog box.

       ●   On the Quick Access toolbar, click **Save** or;

       ●   Select the **File** tab and choose **Save.**

    b.   In the **Save As** dialog box, in the **Table Name** text box, double-click and type the desired name and click **OK.**

Naming Conventions in Access

Many database designers use prefixes as part of every database object's name. Using prefixes is optional, but makes an object's database type immediately obvious. This can be useful to the person who inherits the task of maintaining your database, and can be useful if you resume work on a database after a lapse.

Object	Prefix	Example
Table	tbl	tblSampleTable
Query	qry	qrySampleQuery
Form	frm	frmSampleForm
Subform	fsub	fsubSampleSubform
Report	rpt	rptSampleReport
Subreport	rsub	rsubSampleSubReport

Procedure Reference: Create a Multi-Valued Field

To create a multi-valued field:

1.   Display the desired table in the Design view.

2.   In the document window, for the desired field, click in the **Data Type** column, and from the **Data Type** drop-down list, select **Lookup Wizard.**

3.   In the **Lookup Wizard** dialog box, select the **I will type in the values that I want** option to specify the desired values and click **Next.**

4.   In the list box, specify the necessary values and click **Next.**

5.   Check the **Allow Multiple Values** check box to allow multiple values to be stored in the field and click **Finish.**

6.   Save the table.

Procedure Reference: Display or Hide the Calendar Icon

To display or hide the calendar icon:

1. Display the desired table in the Design view.

2. Select the desired field with a data type of **Date/Time.**

3. In the **Field Properties** pane, on the **General** tab, from the **Show Date Picker** drop-down list, select an option.

   - Select the **For Dates** option to display the calendar icon or;

   - Select the **Never** option to hide the calendar icon.

Procedure Reference: Insert a Record into a Table

To insert a record into a table:

1. Open the desired table.

2. Insert a record.

   a. If necessary, display the table in the Datasheet view.

      - On the **Home** tab, in the **Views** group, click the **View** button or;

      - On the **Home** tab, in the **Views** group, from the **View** drop-down list, select **Datasheet View** or;

      - Right-click the table tab and choose **Datasheet View.**

   b. Add data to a blank record.

      - In the table, in the last row, specify the desired values in the fields.

      - On the **Home** tab, in the **Records** group, click **New,** and in the blank row that is displayed, enter the desired values in the fields.

Saving Table Data

When you enter a value in a table while in Datasheet view, Access automatically saves that table and its new data when you navigate across to another column (field), or another row (record). This allows you to perform data entry tasks without having to save the table after entering each value. This makes Access different from applications like Word or Excel, where all data entered must be saved manually.

Changes to a table's structure (adding, deleting or editing fields) require you to save the table. But changes to a table's content are saved automatically.

Procedure Reference: Insert Fields in a Table

To insert fields in a table:

1. Open a table.

2. Insert a field in the table.

   - Insert a field as the last field in the table in the Datasheet view.

     a. From the **Click to Add** drop-down list, select a data type.

     b. In the inserted column, replace the default field name with the desired field name.

   - Insert a field before another field in the table in the Datasheet view.

     a. Right-click the field before which you want to insert a field and choose **Insert Field.**

     b. Double-click the default field name and type the desired field name.

Fields inserted before another field in the Datasheet view will by default be of the **Text** data type. If the data type is to be modified, switch to the Design view and assign the desired data type.

- Insert a field in the table in the Design view.
  a. Switch to the Design view.
  b. In the document window, insert a field.
    - In the **Field Name** column, in the cell after the existing fields, click and type the desired field name.
    - Right-click the row before which you want to insert a field, choose **Insert Rows,** and in the **Field Name** column, type the desired field name.
    - Select a field before which you want to insert a field, and on the **Design** contextual tab, in the **Tools** group, click **Insert Rows,** and in the **Field Name** column, type the desired field name.
  c. In the document window, for the newly inserted field, click in the **Data Type** column, and from the drop-down list, select the desired data type.

Procedure Reference: Delete Fields in a Table

To delete fields in a table:

1. Open a table.
2. Delete the desired field.
   - Delete a field in the Datasheet view.
     - Right-click a column and choose **Delete Field** or;
     - Select a column, and on the **Home** tab, in the **Records** group, from the **Delete** drop-down list, select **Delete Column** or;
     - Select a column, and on the **Fields** contextual tab, in the **Add & Delete** group, click **Delete.**
   - Delete a field in the Design view.
     - Right-click a row and choose **Delete Rows** or;
     - Click in the desired row, and on the **Design** contextual tab, in the **Tools** group, click **Delete Rows** or;
     - Select the desired row, and on the **Home** tab, in the **Records** group, click **Delete.**
3. In the **Microsoft Access** message box, click **Yes** to confirm deletion.

Procedure Reference: Rename a Field

To rename a field:

1. Open the desired table.
2. Rename the desired field
   - Rename a field in the Datasheet view.
     - Right-click a field, choose **Rename Field,** and type the desired name or;
     - Double-click a field name and type the desired name.
   - In the Design view, double-click a field name and type the desired name.

Procedure Reference: Modify Field Attributes

To modify field attributes:

1. Open a table in the Design view.

2. From the **Data Type** drop-down list of the desired field, select a data type.

3. In the **Description** column, type a description for the desired field.

ACTIVITY 2-2
Creating a Table

Scenario:

Having created a database, you need to store data such as the purchase date, purchase price, warranty, and other information related to the inventory of computers. You decide to create a table to store this data and start inputting the data into the table.

---

1. Create a table.

   a. On the **File** tab, choose **Open.**

   b. In the **Open** dialog box, navigate to the C:\084306Data\Building the Structure of a Database folder and open the MyComputerInventory.accdb database.

   c. Observe that the database is empty and the blank table that was displayed earlier no longer exists.

    When a database is created, a blank table is also automatically created. But if the table is not saved before the database is closed, then the table will no longer exist.

   d. Select the **Create** tab, in the **Tables** group, click **Table** to create a blank table.

   e. On the Quick Access toolbar, click **Save.**

   f. In the **Save As** dialog box, in the **Table Name** text box, type **tblComputers** and click **OK.**

---

2. Add fields to the newly created table.

a.   Right-click the **tblComputers** tab and choose **Design View.**

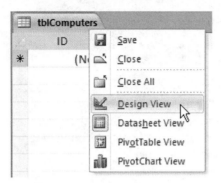

b.   In the tblComputers table, in the **Field Name** column, in the first cell, type *AssetTag* to overwrite the name **ID.**

c.   In the second cell, type *Manufacturer*

d.   In the third cell, type *Date Received*

e.   In the fourth cell, type *Purchase Price*

f.   In the fifth cell, type *Warranty*

3.   Set the data types for the fields in the table.

a.   In the **Data Type** column, observe that the data type for the AssetTag field is set to **AutoNumber.**

b.   For the Date Received field, click in the **Data Type** column, and from the drop-down list, select **Date/Time.**

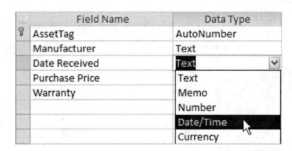

c.   For the Purchase Price field, click in the **Data Type** column, and from the drop-down list, select **Currency.**

d.   For the Warranty field, click in the **Data Type** column, and from the drop-down list, select **Yes/No.**

4.   Create a lookup list for the Manufacturer field.

a. For the Manufacturer field, click in the **Data Type** column, and from the drop-down list, select **Lookup Wizard.**

b. In the **Lookup Wizard,** select the **I will type in the values that I want** option and click **Next.**

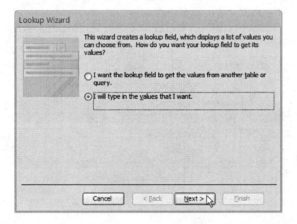

c. In the **Col1** column, in the first cell, click and type *Atlas* and press **Tab.**

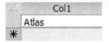

d. In the second cell, type *HiTech* and press **Tab.**

e. In the third cell, type *Micron* and then click **Next.**

f. In the **Do you want to store multiple values for this lookup** section, check the **Allow Multiple Values** check box to allow multiple values to be selected and stored in the field.

g. Click **Finish.**

---

5. Insert a record into the table.

a. Right-click the **tblComputers** tab and choose **Datasheet View.**

b. In the **Microsoft Access** message box, click **Yes.**

---

c. In the Manufacturer column, click in the first cell, and in the lookup list, check the **Atlas** check box.

d. Check the **Micron** check box and click **OK.**

e. In the AssetTag column, verify that the number 1 is displayed. This number displays automatically because the data type of that field is **AutoNumber.**

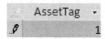

f. In the Date Received column, click in the first cell, and to the right of the Date Received column, click the calendar icon. 🔲

g. Navigate to the date that is six months before the current date.

h. In the Purchase Price column, click and type *8200*

i. In the Warranty column, check the check box.

j. Close the database.

TOPIC C
Manage Tables

You created a table. Although you stored data in a table, there will be instances where you may want to change table properties or rename or delete a table. In this topic, you will manage tables.

When working with a significant volume of data, especially in the business environment, you will undoubtedly need to change or update certain information periodically because information rarely remains static. This may result in the need to modify the tables you created, based on changing needs over time. Access provides a flexible environment to modify tables, as well as set their properties and perform operations such as renaming or deleting tables. By manipulating the properties of tables, you will be able to manage tables dynamically and more efficiently.

The Table Properties Dialog Box

The options in the *Table Properties* dialog box allow you to add a description about a table. The dialog box also displays the date on which the table was created and last modified, and the owner of the table. It also allows you to hide or unhide a table.

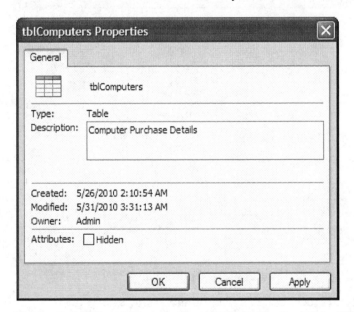

Figure 2-4: The table properties displayed in the Table Properties dialog box.

How to Manage Tables

Procedure Reference: Add a Description to a Table

To add a description to a table:

1. Open the desired database.

2. Open the **<Table Name> Properties** dialog box for the desired table.
   - In the Navigation Pane, right-click the desired table and choose **Table Properties** or;
   - In the Navigation Pane, select the desired table, and on the **Table Tools Design** contextual tab, in the **Show/Hide** group, click **Property Sheet.**

3. In the **<Table Name> Properties** dialog box, in the **Description** text box, type a description of the table.

4. If necessary, in the **Attributes** section, check the **Hidden** check box to hide the table.

5. Click **OK** to close the **<Table Name> Properties** dialog box.

6. If necessary, right-click anywhere in the Navigation Pane and choose **View By→Details** to view the description under the name of the desired table.

 The Navigation Pane allows you to view the details of database objects such as the date when the object was created, the date when it was last modified, and a brief description about the object (if specified).

Procedure Reference: Rename a Table

To rename a table:

1. Open the desired database.

2. In the Navigation Pane, right-click a table and choose **Rename.**

3. In the text box displaying the name of the table, type the desired table name.

4. Click anywhere to deselect the table.

Procedure Reference: Delete a Table

To delete a table:

1. Open the desired database.

2. Delete the desired table.
   - In the Navigation Pane, right-click a table and choose **Delete** or;
   - In the Navigation Pane, select the desired table, and on the **Home** tab, in the **Records** group, click **Delete.**

3. In the **Microsoft Access** message box, click **Yes** to delete the selected table.

Renaming and Deleting Access Objects

The steps you use to rename and delete tables in the Navigation Pane can also be applied to other database objects, such as queries, forms, and reports.

Procedure Reference: Set the Navigation Options

To set the navigation options:

1. In the Navigation Pane, right-click in the blank area and choose **Navigation Options.**

2. Customize the categories in the Navigation Pane.

   ● Add a category.

      a. Click **Add Item** to add a category to the **Categories** list box.

      b. In the **Custom Category** text box, type the desired name.

   ● Delete a category.

      a. Select the desired category and click **Delete Item.**

      b. In the **Microsoft Access** message box, click **OK.**

   ● Rename a category.

      a. Select the desired category and click **Rename Item.**

      b. In the text box containing the category name, type the desired name and press **Enter.**

   ● Reposition a category.

      a. Select a category.

      b. Click the **Move Up** or **Move Down** button to move the category up or down the list of custom categories.

3. Customize the groups in the Navigation Pane.

   ● Add a group.

      a. Click **Add Group** to add a group to the **Groups for <Custom Category>** list box.

      b. In the **Custom Group** text box, type the desired name.

   ● Delete a group.

      a. Select the desired group and click **Delete Group.**

      b. In the **Microsoft Access** message box, click **OK.**

   ● Rename a group.

      a. Select the desired group and click **Rename Group.**

      b. In the text box containing the group name, type the desired name and press **Enter.**

   ● Hide or Unhide a group.

      ● In the **Groups for <Custom Category>** list box, uncheck the check box beside the desired group to hide it in the Navigation Pane.

      ● Check the check box beside the desired group to display it in the Navigation Pane.

   ● Reposition a group.

      a. Select a group.

      b. Click the **Move Up** or **Move Down** button to move the group up or down the list of custom groups.

4. If necessary, in the **Display Options** section, select the desired options.

5. If necessary, in the **Open Objects with** section, select an option to open the objects with a single or double-click.

6. Click **OK.**

ACTIVITY 2-3
Managing Tables in a Database

Data Files:

C:\084306Data\Building the Structure of a Database\OGC Retail.accdb

Scenario:

A colleague has helped you add more tables and data to your database, and has returned a copy to you. While analyzing the tables she added, you realize that the data in a table is out-dated and is no longer needed. You want to rename a table and also want to make the other tables in the database easily recognizable so that you don't need to open them to see what type of data is stored.

---

1. Delete the table containing outdated data.

   a. On the **File** tab, choose **Open.**

   b. In the **Open** dialog box, verify that the C:\084306\Building the Structure of a Database folder is selected and open the OGC Retail.accdb database.

   c. In the Navigation Pane, in the **Tables** section, right-click **tblNotes** and choose **Delete.**

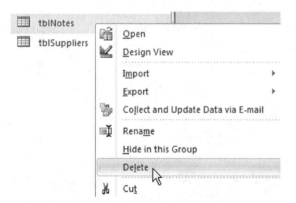

   d. In the **Microsoft Access** message box, click **Yes** to delete the tblNotes table.

   e. Observe that the tblNotes table is deleted from the Navigation Pane.

2. Add a description to a table.

    a.   In the Navigation Pane, right-click **tblComputers** and choose **Table Properties.**

    b.   In the **tblComputers Properties** dialog box, in the **Description** text box, type *Computer Purchase Details* and click **OK.**

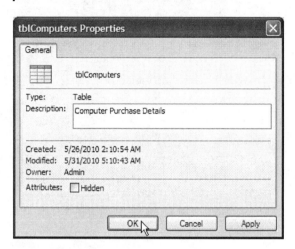

    c.   In the Navigation Pane, below the table names, right-click and choose **View By→Details.**

    d.   Observe that, below the table name tblComputers, the description is displayed along with the created and modified dates.

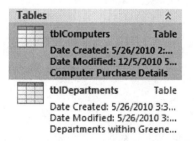

    e.   In the Navigation Pane, below the table names, right-click and choose **View By→List.**

3. Rename a table.

    a.   In the Navigation Pane, right-click **tblSuppliers** and choose **Rename.**

b.   In the text box that displays the table name, type ***tblManufacturers*** and press **Enter.**

c.   Observe that the tables list reordered itself because it is displayed in alphabetical order.

TOPIC D

Establish Table Relationships

You managed tables in a database. While managing tables, you may notice that some tables in the database contain related data, which you will need to view or retrieve together. In this topic, you will create relationships between tables in an Access database.

Before you can realize the full potential of a database for querying, generating reports, and updating data, you need to link the tables of the database. For example, when you enter data in a table, there is the risk that you might forget to make related changes across other tables, resulting in data inconsistency. Setting table relationships right at the start will help ensure that the correct data is stored across all the related tables in the database.

Join Lines

Definition:

A *join line* is a line drawn between a field of one table and the related field of another to indicate that the two tables are related by fields in the tables. Each end of the join line will display either the number 1 or an infinity symbol. This denotes the kind of relationship, such as one-to-one or one-to-many, between the two tables.

Example:

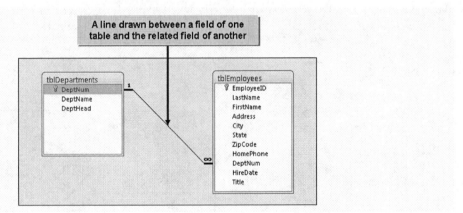

Figure 2-5: The join lines indicating the relationship between fields in tables.

The Relationships Window

The *Relationships window* displays relationships between various tables in a database. If no relationships are defined and you are opening the Relationships window for the first time, Access prompts you to add a table or query to the window. The Relationships window displays tables as field lists and also displays the join lines between related tables.

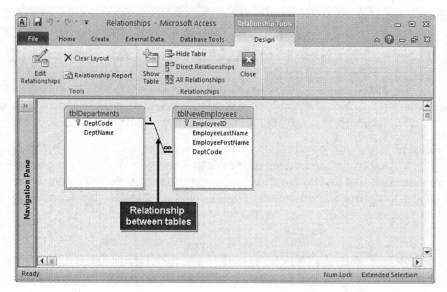

Figure 2-6: The Relationships window displaying the relationship between two tables.

Referential Integrity

Definition:

A database is said to have *referential integrity* when every foreign key in every table has a link to a primary key in another table. Ensuring referential integrity disallows the entry of invalid data.

Example:

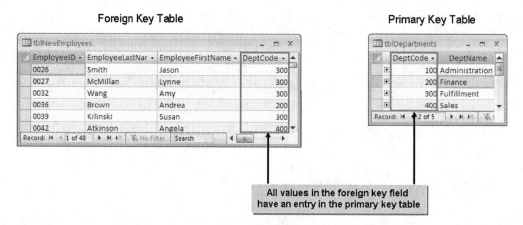

Figure 2-7: Tables displaying referential integrity of data.

Analogy:

An employee cannot belong to a department that does not exist. The Departments table contains all the existing departments. You need to ensure that all the values in the foreign key field in the Employees table have a corresponding value in the primary key field of the Departments table.

Guidelines to Enforce Referential Integrity

Enforcing referential integrity for a relationship can avoid the loss or inadvertent updating of data.

Guidelines

Referential integrity between two tables can be enforced by following these guidelines.

- When adding a record to a table with a foreign key, ensure that a corresponding record exists in the primary key table.

- When updating a foreign key in a table with a value, ensure that the value is present in the primary key table.

- When deleting a record from the primary key table, ensure that no linked records exist in another table.

Example:

The CustomerID field in a customers table is a unique primary key and can be related to a CustomerID field in an orders table in a one-to-many relationship. You do not want to allow a user to enter a customer in the orders table when there is no record for that customer in the customers table. Nor do you want the user to alter the CustomerID field for a record in the customers table because that would break the link with the related orders data for that customer. Deleting a customer record that has matching order records is also not allowed. This is an ideal situation for enforcing referential integrity.

The Edit Relationships Dialog Box

The *Edit Relationships* dialog box allows you to change a table relationship. Using this dialog box, you can change the tables or queries involved on either side of the relationship and also specify the fields that are related. It also allows you to specify the properties of the relationship and create new relationships.

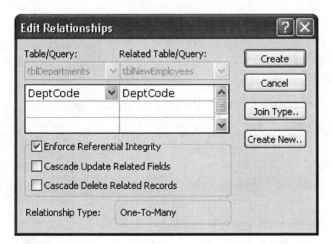

Figure 2-8: *The Edit Relationships dialog box displaying options to modify an existing table relationship.*

You can set options in the **Edit Relationships** dialog box to enforce referential integrity.

Option	Description
Enforce Referential Integrity	Ensures that you will not be able to enter a value in the foreign key table field if a corresponding value does not exist in the primary key table field.
Cascade Delete Related Records	Ensures that if you delete a record from a primary key table and if matching records exist in a related table, the matching records in the related table are also deleted.
Cascade Update Related Fields	Ensures that if you make changes to a primary key table field and if matching records exist in related tables, the values in the related tables are also updated.

Relationship Reports

A *relationship report* is used to print table relationships. You can view the relationship report by clicking the **Relationship Report** button in the **Tools** group on the **Design** contextual tab. In the Relationship Report view, the **Print Preview** tab is enabled. Using the options on the tab, you can set the page size and margins, set the report page layout, view a document as desired, export the data to another application, and print the page.

How to Create a Table Relationship

Procedure Reference: Create a Table Relationship

To create a table relationship:

1. On the Ribbon, select the **Database Tools** tab.
2. On the **Database Tools** tab, in the **Relationships** group, click **Relationships** to display the Relationships window.
3. Display the **Show Table** dialog box.
   - On the **Design** contextual tab, in the **Relationships** group, click **Show Table** or;
   - In the Relationships window, right-click anywhere and choose **Show Table.**
4. In the **Show Table** dialog box, on the **Tables** tab, select the desired tables.
5. Click **Add** to add the selected tables to the Relationships window.
6. Click **Close** to close the **Show Table** dialog box.
7. In the Relationships window, in the desired table, click the desired field and drag it to the matching field in another table to create a relationship.
8. In the **Edit Relationships** dialog box, check the desired check boxes to enforce referential integrity.
9. Click **Create** to establish a relationship between the two tables.

Procedure Reference: Edit a Table Relationship

To edit a table relationship:

1. On the Ribbon, select the **Database Tools** tab.
2. On the **Database Tools** tab, in the **Relationships** group, click **Relationships** to display the Relationships window.

3. Display the **Edit Relationships** dialog box.

- On the **Design** contextual tab, in the **Tools** group, click **Edit Relationships** or;
- In the Relationships window, double-click a join line.

4. In the **Edit Relationships** dialog box, select the desired table or query and specify the related fields.

5. If necessary, select the desired options to enforce referential integrity.

6. Click **Create** to display the edited relationship.

Procedure Reference: Print Table Relationships

To print table relationships:

1. On the Ribbon, select the **Database Tools** tab.

2. On the **Database Tools** tab, in the **Relationships** group, click **Relationships** to display the Relationships window.

3. On the **Design** contextual tab, in the **Tools** group, click **Relationship Report** to display the table relationships in the form of a report.

4. Save the table relationship report.

   a. Select the **File** tab and choose **Save As** to display the **Save As** dialog box.

   b. If necessary, in the **Save As** dialog box, in the **Report Name** text box, type a name for the report.

   c. In the **Save As** dialog box, click **OK.**

5. On the **Print Preview** tab, click **Print,** and in the **Print** dialog box, specify the desired settings and click **OK** to print the relationship report.

ACTIVITY 2-4
Creating a Table Relationship

Before You Begin:

The OGC Retail.accdb file is open.

Scenario:

You have stored all the required data in different tables in a database. The Employee table contains details about the employees and the Department table contains department information. Each employee belongs to a department and you want to relate these two tables so that you can efficiently retrieve information from across the tables as necessary. You also want to take a printout of the relationship report.

1. Display the required tables in the Relationships window.

   a. Select the **Database Tools** tab, and in the **Relationships** group, click **Relationships** to display the Relationships window.

   b. On the **Design** contextual tab, in the **Relationships** group, click **Show Table.**

   c. In the **Show Table** dialog box, verify that the **Tables** tab is selected and then select **tblDepartments.**

   d. Hold down **Ctrl** and select **tblEmployees.**

   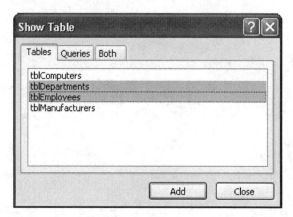

   e. Click **Add** to add the selected tables to the Relationships window and click **Close.**

2. Create a table relationship.

   a. In the Relationships window, in the tblEmployees field list, scroll down to display the DeptNum field.

   b. In the tblDepartments field list, click and drag the **DeptNum** field to the DeptNum field in the tblEmployees field list.

   c. In the **Edit Relationships** dialog box, check the **Enforce Referential Integrity** check box to enforce referential integrity in the relationship and click **Create.**

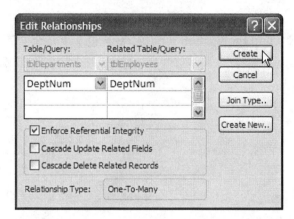

   d. In the Relationships window, observe that a join line connecting the DeptNum fields in the two tables is displayed.

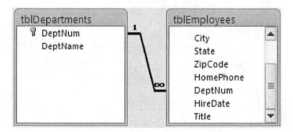

   e. On the Quick Access toolbar, click the **Save** button to save the relationship.

3. Print a relationship report.

   a. On the **Design** contextual tab, in the **Tools** group, click **Relationship Report.**

   b. Observe that the table relationship is displayed in the form of a report and the **Print Preview** tab is displayed on the Ribbon.

   c. Select the **File** tab and choose **Save Object As.**

   d. In the **Save As** dialog box, in the **Save 'Report1' to** text box, type *rptDeptEmployees* and click **OK.**

   e. Select the **Print Preview** tab, and in the **Print** group, click **Print.**

   f. In the **Print** dialog box, click **OK** to print the relationship report.

   g. Close the Relationships for OGC Retail and Relationships windows, and then close the database.

Lesson 2 Follow-up

In this lesson, you built the structure of a database. Although, using an existing template for a database or table can save you time and effort, creating a database from scratch will give you the flexibility to organize data as desired.

1. **Give examples of fields that you will define when creating tables.**

2. **Which Access feature would you use most often when creating a database?**

3 | Managing Data in a Table

Lesson Time: 1 hour(s)

Lesson Objectives:

In this lesson, you will manage data in tables.

You will:

- Modify table data.
- Sort and filter records.
- View data from related tables.

Introduction

You created a database using Access and also built the basic table structure. You may now have to ensure that data is stored in these tables to meet the objectives the database was built for. In this lesson, you will manage table data.

Information in a database is dynamic. As it keeps changing, you need to make corresponding changes to your database. To do that, you might want to locate the desired data quickly. Access provides you with various tools to easily add, locate, and view data.

TOPIC A
Modify Table Data

You created the basic table structure within a database. To keep data in these tables current, you need to know how to add, delete, and update data in a table. In this topic, you will modify table data.

Updating information is one of the most important tasks you will perform with your databases. A database that is incomplete or that contains outdated records is not a reliable source of information. Adding new records and deleting old ones will help to keep the data in your tables reliable.

The Find and Replace Dialog Box

The **Find and Replace** dialog box can be used to quickly locate and change database information. The dialog box contains two tabs with options that help you to search for and replace data.

Tab	Allows You To
Find	Specify the text to be located in the **Find What** text box, the search target, and the direction in which the search should proceed.
Replace	Specify the text to be located in the **Replace With** text box, the text with which the located data should be replaced, the search target, and the direction in which the search should proceed.

The Record Navigation Bar

The *Record Navigation bar* in the Datasheet view helps you navigate through a recordset. You can navigate to the previous, next, first, or last record in a recordset by using the controls on the Record Navigation bar. You can also use the **Search** text box to quickly navigate to a record containing specific data and use the **Filtered** button to remove a filter that is applied to a field in a table.

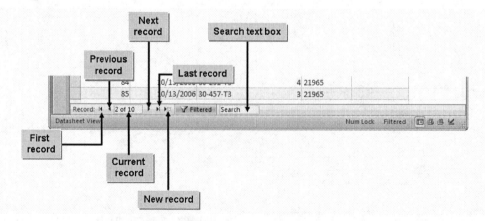

Figure 3-1: *The navigation options on the Record Navigation bar.*

The Totals Command

The *Totals command* is used to add a **Total** row to a table. In the **Total** row, you can display a value that is calculated from all the values in a specified field. The displayed value can be the sum, average, standard deviation, or variance of the values in a field. You can also display a count of records and the maximum or minimum value stored in a field.

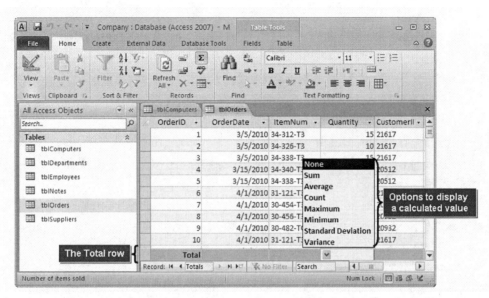

Figure 3-2: *A Total row added to a table.*

How to Modify Table Data

Procedure Reference: Delete a Record from a Table

To delete a record from a table:

1. Open the desired table.
2. Select the record to be deleted.
3. Delete the selected record.
   - On the **Home** tab, in the **Records** group, from the **Delete** drop-down list, select **Delete Record** or;
   - Right-click the selected record and choose **Delete Record** or;
   - Press **Delete.**

Procedure Reference: Update Data in a Table

To update data in a table:

1. Open the desired table.
2. Navigate to a record and select the value in a desired field.
3. Type an appropriate value in the field to update the record.
4. Save the changes made to the record.
   - Click in any field of a different record or;
   - Save the table.

Procedure Reference: Find Data in a Record

To find data in a record:

1. Open the desired table.

2. Open the **Find and Replace** dialog box.

    - On the **Home** tab, in the **Find** group, click **Find** or;

    - Press **Ctrl+F.**

3. In the **Find and Replace** dialog box, on the **Find** tab, in the **Find What** text box, type the text or value that you want to find.

4. If necessary, from the **Look In** drop-down list, select an option.

    - Select **Current field** to search only in the current field.

    - Select **Current document** to search in the current document only.

5. If necessary, from the **Match** drop-down list, select an option.

    - Select **Any Part of Field** to match the search text with any part of or complete field values.

    - Select **Whole Field** to match the search text with the entire field values.

    - Select **Start of Field** to match the search text with only the starting characters of field values.

6. If necessary, from the **Search** drop-down list, select an option.

    - Select **Up** to search in records that precede the selected row in the table.

    - Select **Down** to search in records that follow the selected row in the table.

    - Select **All** to search in records throughout the table.

7. If necessary, check the **Match Case** check box to search for field values that match the casing of the search text.

8. If necessary, check the **Search Fields As Formatted** check box to search for field values that have the input mask set.

9. Click **Find Next** to find text that matches the text specified in the **Find What** text box.

10. If necessary, click **Find Next** repeatedly to find further occurrences of the search text.

11. In the **Find and Replace** dialog box, click **Close.**

Procedure Reference: Replace Data in a Record

To replace data in a record:

1. Display the **Replace** tab.

    - On the **Home** tab, in the **Find** group, click **Replace** or;

    - On the **Home** tab, in the **Find** group, click **Find** and select the **Replace** tab or;

    - Press **Ctrl+H.**

2. In the **Find and Replace** dialog box, on the **Replace** tab, in the **Find What** text box, type the text you want to replace.

3. If necessary, set the search options.

4. On the **Replace** tab, in the **Replace With** text box, type the text with which you want to replace the existing text.

5. Replace the text with the text specified in the **Replace With** text box.

   ● Click **Replace** to replace the selected instance of the search criteria.

   ● Click **Replace All** to replace every instance of the search criteria with the new text.

6. In the **Find and Replace** dialog box, click **Close.**

7. Save the table.

Procedure Reference: Add a Total Row to a Table

To add a **Total** row to a table:

1. Open the desired table.

2. On the **Home** tab, in the **Records** group, click **Totals** to add a **Total** row at the end of the table.

3. In the **Total** row, click the cell for a field for which you need to add a total value, and from the displayed drop-down list, select an option.

   ● Select **Sum** to obtain the sum of the values in a column.

   ● Select **Average** to obtain the average of the values in a column.

   ● Select **Count** to count the number of values in a column.

   ● Select **Standard Deviation** to obtain the standard deviation of the values in a column.

   ● Select **Variance** to obtain the variance of the values in a column.

   ● Select **Maximum** to obtain the maximum value in a column.

   ● Select **Minimum** to obtain the minimum value in a column.

4. Save the table.

The Appearance of the Total Row

The **Total** row is displayed below the records of a table in the Datasheet view. If the number of records exceeds that of rows that can be displayed in the window, then the **Total** row appears just above the Record Navigation bar.

Adding an Alternate Row Color

You can set an alternate background color for each row of a table by using the **Alternate Row Color** command in the **Text Formatting** group on the **Home** tab.

ACTIVITY 3-1
Modifying Data in a Table

Data Files:

C:\084306Data\Managing Data in a Table\OGC Retail.accdb

Scenario:

Your coworker is working on the database that you created and has added more tables to store details of manufacturers, departments, employees, and orders. He has also included data in the newly added tables.

Now, you need to include the details of the new computers that were purchased recently and also update the Employee table to store information for a new employee. Also, owing to a Human Resources department initiative, you want to make sure that the titles of employees designated as Sales Representative are changed to Sales Executive. You also want to update the contact details for one of the employees and delete the information of an employee who has left the organization.

The database also contains a table with information on customer purchase orders. You want to view the total quantity ordered by all the customers.

1. Add a new employee record to the tblEmployees table.

   a. On the **File** tab, click **Open.**

   b. Navigate to the C:\084306Data\Managing Data in a Table folder and open the OGC Retail.accdb database.

   c. Double-click the **tblEmployees** table to display it.

   d. On the **Home** tab, in the **Records** group, click **New.**

   e. Observe that a new row is added after the last record in the table.

   f. In the blank record that is inserted, in the EmployeeID field, type **0143** and press **Enter.**

   g. In the LastName field, type **Smith** and press **Enter.**

   h. In the FirstName field, type **Pat** and press **Enter.**

   i. Similarly, in the Address, City, State, and ZipCode fields, type **127 Larkspur Lane**, **Potter**, **OH**, and **72057**, respectively.

   j. In the HomePhone, DeptNum, HireDate, and Title fields, type **5095553254**, **400**, **8/12/2010**, and **Human Resources Benefits Specialist,** respectively.

k. Press **Enter** to move the insertion point to the next row and save the changes in the table.

2. Replace all the instances of the text "Sales Representative" with "Sales Executive."

 a. On the **Home** tab, in the **Find** group, click the **Replace** button.

 b. In the **Find and Replace** dialog box, on the **Replace** tab, in the **Find What** text box, type **Sales Representative** and press **Tab.**

 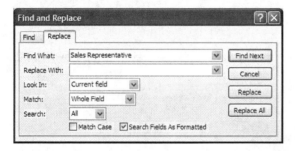

 c. In the **Replace With** text box, type **Sales Executive**

 d. From the **Look In** drop-down list, select **Current document.**

 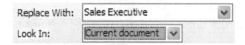

 e. Click **Replace All** to replace all the instances of the text "Sales Representative" with the text "Sales Executive."

 f. In the **Microsoft Access** message box, click **Yes.**

 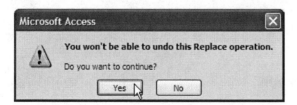

 g. In the **Find and Replace** dialog box, click the **Close** button.

3. Update an employee record.

 a. On the Record Navigation bar, in the **Search** text box, click and type **0051**

b.   Observe that the record with an EmployeeID value of 0051 is selected and scroll to the right.

c.   In the HomePhone column of the selected record, double-click **5011** to select the last four digits of the phone number and type *5267*

d.   Scroll to the left to view the EmployeeID column.

4.   Delete an employee record from the table.

a.   Move the mouse pointer to the left of EmployeeID 0026 and when it changes to an arrow, click to select the record.

b.   On the **Home** tab, in the **Records** group, from the **Delete** drop-down list, select **Delete Record.**

c.   In the **Microsoft Access** message box, click **Yes.**

d.   In the document window, click the **Close** button to close the tblEmployees table.

5.   Add a **Total** row to the tblOrders table.

a.   In the Navigation Pane, double-click **tblOrders** to open the table.

b.   On the **Home** tab, in the **Records** group, click **Totals.**

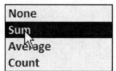

c.   Observe that a **Total** row is displayed above the Record Navigation bar.

d.   In the **Total** row, click the **Quantity** column, and from the drop-down list, select **Sum.**

e. Observe that the result displayed is 805, which is the sum of all the values in the Quantity column.

f. On the Quick Access toolbar, click the **Save** button to save the table with the **Total** row.

TOPIC B
Sort and Filter Records

You modified data in a table. In a large table, locating records may be difficult if the records are not displayed in the desired sequence or if the records with similar or related data are not grouped together. In this topic, you will sort and filter records.

It is difficult to find specific data in a database that has a number of large tables. Organizing data in a specific order, such as by ascending or descending values, can help you locate information quickly. Also, database tables usually store broad categories of information from which you may need to cull records with related data. Access provides you with options to sort and filter records to simplify the process and reduce the time you spend in searching.

Sorting

Definition:

Sorting is a method of arranging data in a specific order. Data in Access can be sorted in either ascending or descending order based on numeric or alphabetic information. You can sort data from the smallest to the largest or from the largest to the smallest values based on the numeric values in a field. You can also sort data ranging from the oldest to the newest or from the newest to the oldest based on dates stored in a date type of field. An applied sort can be removed when not required.

Example:

Figure 3-3: A table displaying records sorted in ascending order.

Sorting Records Based on Multiple Fields

Access allows you to sort records based on two or more fields simultaneously. To sort records based on multiple fields, the fields must be arranged adjacent to each other so that they can be selected together. The first field in the selection is considered the primary sort field and the others are considered the secondary sort fields. This means that the records will be arranged in the desired order according to the primary field first. For records with identical values in that field, the secondary fields will be used to determine the sort order for those records.

The Filter Feature

In Access, you can *filter* data based on the criteria applied to values in a column. You can filter data to display only the records that match your criteria. You can apply filters such as text filters for the text data type, number filters for the number data type, and date filters for the date data type. When you apply a filter to a column that is already filtered, the existing filter is removed. However, it is possible to specify a different filter for each field displayed in the table; that is, multiple filters can be applied to a table at the same time.

Filter Options

The **Sort & Filter** group provides you with options to filter records in a table based on your requirements.

Option	*Allows You To*
The **Selection** drop-down list	Filter items depending on the data value in a selected field. There are a number of options available in the drop-down list and these options filter data based on the values the field contains, based on the values the field does not contain, or based on the values between a particular range. If you want to filter items based on a date field, the **Selection** drop-down list provides options to select records with values before or after a specific date or even values within a range of dates.
The **Advanced** drop-down list	Apply filters that are not commonly available in the filters list or save a filter as a query object in a database.
The **Toggle Filter** button	Switch between a filtered and an unfiltered view of data in a table.

Saving Filtered Data as a Query or Table

Access retains a filter only when a table is open. When you close a table and later decide to use the filter again, you will need to create the filter again from scratch. To avoid this, Access allows you to save filtered data as a query or table. In the **Save As** dialog box, you can type a name for the query or table and select the desired object type from the **As** drop-down list and then click **OK.**

How to Sort and Filter Records

Procedure Reference: Sort Records in a Table According to a Field

To sort records in a table according to a field:

1. Open the desired table.
2. In the table, select the field by which you need to sort the table.
3. Sort the table.

   - Sort the table in ascending order.

     ■ On the **Home** tab, in the **Sort & Filter** group, click **Ascending** or;

     ■ In the table header of the desired field, from the drop-down list, select **Sort A To Z.**

   - Sort the table in descending order.

     ■ On the **Home** tab, in the **Sort & Filter** group, click **Descending** or;

     ■ In the table header of the desired field, from the drop-down list, select **Sort Z To A.**

4. If necessary, on the **Home** tab, in the **Sort & Filter** group, click **Remove Sort** to restore the records to the original order.
5. Save the table.

Procedure Reference: Rearrange Fields in a Table

To rearrange fields in a table:

1. Open a table in Datasheet view.
2. Click a column heading to select that field.
3. Drag the column to the right or to the left to move the column.

Procedure Reference: Sort Records in a Table According to Two or More Fields

To sort records in a table according to two or more fields:

1. Open the desired table.
2. If necessary, rearrange the columns in the table so that the desired sort fields are adjacent to each other and can be selected together.
3. Select the fields that need to be sorted. The first field from the left will be the primary sort field and the following fields will be the secondary sort fields.
4. Sort the table in ascending or descending order.
5. If necessary, on the **Home** tab, in the **Sort & Filter** group, click **Remove Sort** to restore the records to the original order.
6. Save the table.

Procedure Reference: Filter Records in a Table

To filter records in a table:

1. Open the desired table.
2. Select the data to be filtered by column.
3. On the **Home** tab, in the **Sort & Filter** group, click **Filter.**
4. From the displayed drop-down list, select the values to filter the data as you desire and click **OK.**

Procedure Reference: Save an Object as Other Objects

To save an object as other Access objects:

1. Select the **File** tab and choose **Save Object As.**

2. In the **Save As** dialog box, specify the object name and type and then click **OK.**

Procedure Reference: Remove a Filter

To remove a filter:

1. Select the column from which you need to remove the applied filter.

2. Remove the filter to display all the records in the table.

   - Remove the filter by using the **Filter** drop-down list.

     a. On the **Home** tab, in the **Sort & Filter** group, click **Filter.**

     b. In the displayed drop-down list, check the **Select All** check box and click **OK.**

   - To the right of the name of the filtered column, click the filter icon, and from the displayed drop-down list, select **Clear Filter From [Column Name]** or;

   - On the **Home** tab, in the **Sort & Filter** group, click **Toggle Filter** or;

   - On the Record Navigation bar, click **Filtered.**

Procedure Reference: Hide or Unhide Fields

To hide or unhide fields:

1. Open the desired table in the Datasheet view.

2. Hide the desired fields.

   - Right-click a field and choose **Hide Fields** or;

   - Select a field, and on the **Home** tab, in the **Records** group, from the **More** drop-down list, select **Hide Fields.**

3. If necessary, unhide the desired fields.

   1. Display the **Unhide Columns** dialog box.

      - Right-click a field and choose **Unhide Fields** or;

      - On the **Home** tab, in the **Records** group, from the **More** drop-down list, select **Unhide Fields.**

   2. In the **Unhide Columns** dialog box, check the check boxes of the desired fields you want to unhide and click **Close.**

Procedure Reference: Freeze or Unfreeze Fields

To freeze or unfreeze fields:

1. Open the desired table in the Datasheet view.

2. Freeze the desired fields.

   - Right-click a field and choose **Freeze Fields** or;

   - Select a field, and on the **Home** tab, in the **Records** group, from the **More** drop-down list, select **Freeze Fields.**

3. If necessary unfreeze all the fields.

   - Right-click a field and choose **Unfreeze All Fields** or;

   - On the **Home** tab, in the **Records** group, from the **More** drop-down list, select **Unfreeze All Fields.**

ACTIVITY 3-2
Sorting Records in a Table

Before You Begin:

The OGC Retail.accdb file is open.

Scenario:

All customer orders are maintained in the tblOrders table. Your sales manager wants to know how many orders were placed by the customers, Household Helper and Zilinski's Home Store. But to retrieve order details, you will first need to retrieve the customer IDs of the customers from the tblCustomers table. You also want to analyze the orders placed by SuperSaver to check their eligibility for a new discount scheme the company is planning.

1. Retrieve the customer IDs for the customers whose orders you want to check.

    a. In the Navigation Pane, double-click **tblCustomers** to open the table.

    b. Observe that the CustomerID number in the Household Helper record is 20151 and in the Zilinski's Home Store record, 21965. Also, observe that the customer ID corresponding to SuperSaver is 20493.

CustomerII ▾	CustomerName ▾
20151	Household Helper
20181	Breck's Hardware
20493	SuperSaver
20512	Spring Cleaning Co.
20657	Johnson's Janitorial Service
20688	Dazzle Florists
20784	Schilling Home Supply
20926	The Value Store
20932	Somerville Hardware
21510	Marlene's Cleaning Service
21570	Home & Hardware
21587	Clarkson Cleaning
21617	S-Mart Home Emporium
21965	Zilinski's Home Store

    c. Close the table.

2. Sort the tblOrders table in ascending order to locate the orders placed by Household Helper with ease.

    a. In the tblOrders table, in the CustomerID column, click any field.

b. On the **Home** tab, in the **Sort & Filter** group, click **Ascending.**

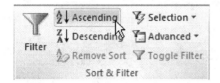

c. Observe that the first three records are for the CustomerID 20151, which is the CustomerID for HouseHold Helper.

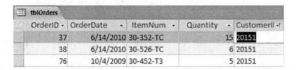

3. Sort the table in descending order to display the orders placed by Zilinski's Home Store at the top of the table.

a. On the **Home** tab, in the **Sort & Filter** group, click **Descending.**

b. Observe that the first 10 records are for the CustomerID 21965, which is the CustomerID for Zilinski's Home Store.

ItemNum	▾	Quantity	▾	CustomerI ▾
30-457-T3		3		21965
30-231-T3		4		21965
30-457-T3		3		21965
30-454-T3		3		21965
30-452-T3		3		21965
34-312-T3		8		21965
34-326-T3		12		21965
31-122-T3		15		21965
34-340-T3		15		21965
31-121-T3		20		21965

4. Clear all the sorting applied to the table.

a. On the **Home** tab, in the **Sort & Filter** group, click **Remove Sort.**

b. Observe that the records in the table are restored to their original order.

5. Filter the orders placed by SuperSaver.

a. Click the **CustomerID** column header.

b.   On the **Home** tab, in the **Sort & Filter** group, click **Filter.**

c.   In the displayed drop-down list, uncheck the **Select All** check box.

d.   Check the **20493** check box and click **OK.**

e.   Observe that only the rows with the CustomerID 20493 are displayed.

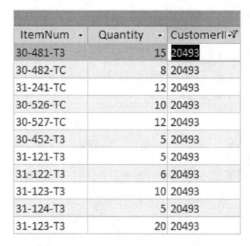

---

6.   Count the number of orders placed by SuperSaver.

    a.   In the **Total** row, in the Quantity column, click in the cell, and from the drop-down list, select **Count.**

b. Observe that the result displayed is 11, which is the count of the records with the CustomerID 20493.

Quantity	CustomerII
15	20493
8	20493
12	20493
10	20493
12	20493
5	20493
5	20493
6	20493
10	20493
5	20493
20	20493
0	
11	

c. On the Quick Access toolbar, click **Save.**

 Only the addition of the **Total** row is saved. The filter is not saved.

d. Close the tblOrders table.

TOPIC C
Work with Subdatasheets

You sorted and filtered data to view data in a table with ease. Sometimes, you may need to view data from another table along with the data from a table you are working on. In this topic, you will work with subdatasheets.

Understanding and knowing how Access tables are related and evaluating the relationships between tables is a great starting point. But if you are working with one table and you need to view related data in another table, how can you display it? Subdatasheets in Access allow you to view related data from another table for any record.

Subdatasheets

When a table is opened in a database, it can be displayed as a datasheet with data arranged in rows and columns. A *subdatasheet* is a datasheet that is nested within another datasheet and contains data related to the first datasheet. When a record has a subdatasheet, it is indicated by a plus sign in the left column of the datasheet. Clicking the plus sign displays the subdatasheet, with the related data. A minus sign in the left column indicates that a subdatasheet is open.

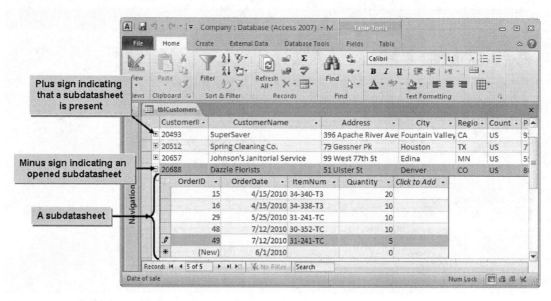

Figure 3-4: *Data in a subdatasheet.*

How to View Data from Related Tables

Procedure Reference: Create a Subdatasheet

To create a subdatasheet:

1. Open the desired table.
2. In the **Records** group, click the **More** drop-down arrow, and from the displayed drop-down list, select **Subdatasheet→Subdatasheet.**
3. In the **Insert Subdatasheet** dialog box, select a related table from which data is to be displayed and click **OK.**
4. In the **Microsoft Access** message box, click **Yes.**

Procedure Reference: View Data in a Subdatasheet

To view data in a subdatasheet:

1. Open the desired table with a subdatasheet.
2. To the left of the record you need to view, click the plus sign to expand the subdatasheet and view the related data.
3. If necessary, to the left of the record, click the minus sign to collapse the subdatasheet.

Procedure Reference: Modify Data in a Subdatasheet

To modify data in a subdatasheet:

1. To the left of the record you need to modify, click the plus sign to expand the subdatasheet and view the related data.
2. Select a value in a field.
3. Type the desired value to replace the selected value.
4. If necessary, to the left of the record, click the minus sign to collapse the subdatasheet.

ACTIVITY 3-3
Modifying Data in a Subdatasheet

Before You Begin:

The OGC Retail.accdb file is open.

Scenario:

All customer orders are maintained in the tblOrders table in the company database. Because this table contains only the customer ID for each order and not the customer name, you find it difficult to match orders to customers. You feel that if you can view all the orders pertaining to a customer, your understanding of order patterns will improve. You also want to change the quantity ordered for OrderID 15 from the customer, Dazzle Florists, but do not want to open multiple tables to find this information and make the change.

---

1. Add a subdatasheet.

    a. In the Navigation Pane, double-click **tblCustomers** to open the table.

    b. In the tblCustomers table, observe that the field with the CustomerID 20151 is selected.

    c. On the **Home** tab, in the **Records** group, click the **More** drop-down arrow, and from the displayed list, select **Subdatasheet→Subdatasheet.**

    d. In the **Insert Subdatasheet** dialog box, on the **Tables** tab, select **tblOrders** and click **OK.**

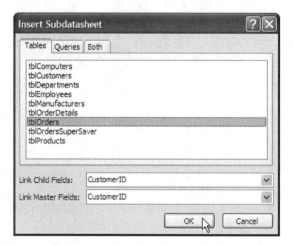

e. Observe that a plus sign (+) appears for each record in the column to the left of the CustomerID column.

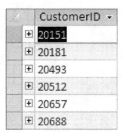

2. View the number of orders placed by a customer.

a. To the left of CustomerID 20151, click the plus sign (+) to expand the subdatasheet.

b. Observe that the plus sign changes to a minus sign indicating that the corresponding subdatasheet is expanded, and in the subdatasheet, observe that three orders are listed for the customer "Household Helper."

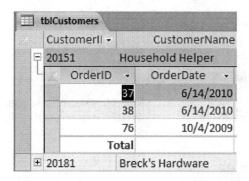

c. To the left of CustomerID 20688, click the plus sign (+) to expand the subdatasheet.

    d.   Observe that both the subdatasheets that you opened remain open at the same time.

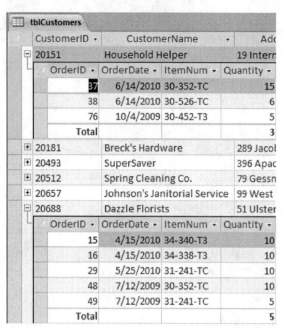

3.   Modify the data in a subdatasheet and verify the change.

    a.   In the subdatasheet for CustomerID 20688, for the record that has the OrderID 15, in the Quantity column, double-click the value **10**, type *20* and press **Enter.**

    b.   Click **Save** to commit the change.

    c.   In the Navigation Pane, double-click **tblOrders** to display the table.

    d.   Observe that for the CustomerID 20688, in the record with the OrderID 15, the quantity is changed to 20.

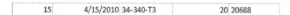

    e.   Close the tblOrders table.

    f.   Close the tblCustomers table.

    g.   Close the database.

Lesson 3 Follow-up

In this lesson, you managed data in tables. With Access, you can update data in tables and sort and filter records from related tables to locate and view data with ease.

1. **Which Access feature for managing tables is the most useful to you?**

2. **What are the instances when you will need to sort or filter records?**

4 | Querying a Database

Lesson Time: 1 hour(s)

Lesson Objectives:

In this lesson, you will query a database.

You will:

- Create a query.
- Add criteria to a query.
- Add a calculated field to a query.
- Perform calculations on a record group.

Introduction

You located data in tables to find necessary information. Sometimes, you may have to perform more complex data retrieval tasks to display records that meet specific criteria. In this lesson, you will create queries to retrieve information.

Unless you have a mechanism for isolating and extracting data, looking for specific information in a database will be like looking for a needle in a haystack. A database is helpful only when you can retrieve data from it as easily as you can add data to it. Knowing how to retrieve information from a table or multiple tables will greatly reduce the time it takes to present meaningful information based on the data.

TOPIC A
Create a Query

You viewed data from a table while working on another related table. Often, you may need to collate data from multiple tables. In this topic, you will create queries to retrieve data from related tables.

There may be instances where you need to retrieve relevant information from different tables at the same time; for instance, you may have to identify employees who come under a specific department and analyze their payroll from the database. You can get such information by creating queries that allow you to retrieve data from multiple tables. You can also save and store the queries as reusable objects in Access.

The Simple Query Wizard

The *Simple Query Wizard* allows you to create a query by following a step-by-step guided approach. You can select tables and queries available in a database from which you want to query data. Depending on the table or query you choose, the **Available Fields** list box displays a list of fields from which you can select the fields to be included in your query. The output of the **Simple Query Wizard** is displayed as a query object in the Navigation Pane.

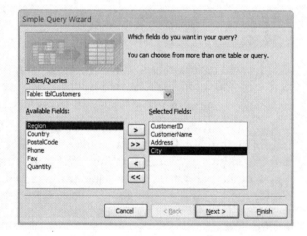

Figure 4-1: *The Simple Query Wizard displaying fields selected for a query.*

Types of Queries

You can create several types of queries by using the **Query Wizard** dialog box.

Query Type	Enables You To
Simple	Select fields from multiple tables and queries.
Crosstab	Calculate and summarize table data in a spreadsheet like format.
Find Duplicates	Find duplicate field values in a table or query result.
Find Unmatched	Find records in one table or query that have no related records in another table or query result.

Query Object Views

A query object can be displayed in different views in Access. For each view, the **Design** contextual tab is displayed with commands to manipulate the query in the displayed view.

Query View	Allows You To
Datasheet	Display the query result in a table similar to a spreadsheet.
PivotTable	Create PivotTables from the query result.
PivotChart	Create PivotCharts from the query result.
SQL	Write SQL query statements.
Design	Build a query by adding fields and conditions.

The Query Design Feature

The *Query Design* feature allows you to create a query in the Design view. You can add the required tables and queries to the Design view. From the field lists of the tables and queries, you can add fields to the query design grid. You can also specify the criteria, sort orders, and commands to summarize information retrieved by the query.

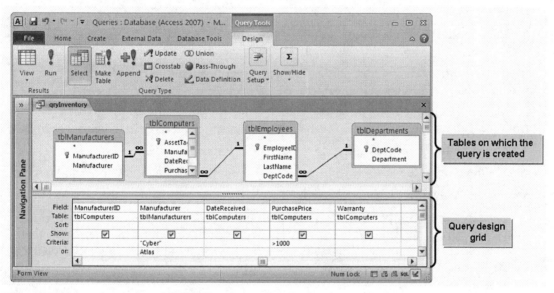

Figure 4-2: *A query created using the Query Design feature.*

The groups on the **Design** contextual tab assist you in creating and modifying queries.

Group	Enables You To
Results	Change the view and execute a query.
Query Type	Specify the query types that can be used to select, append, update, or delete records. It also has SQL-specific options and an option for creating a crosstab query.

Group	Enables You To
Query Setup	Insert and delete rows and columns, launch the **Expression Builder** for building expressions, and launch the **Show Table** dialog box for setting up a query from a table, another query, or both.
Show/Hide	Show or hide tables, add the **Total** row to the query design grid, display the **Property Sheet** pane and the **Query Parameters** dialog box, and hide or unhide the table names displayed in the query design grid.

The Run Command

The *Run command* is used to execute a query from the Design view. You can click the **Run** button in the **Results** group on the **Design** contextual tab to execute a query. You can also run a query by double-clicking it in the Navigation Pane.

How to Create a Query

Procedure Reference: Create a Select Query Using the Query Wizard

To create a select query using the **Query Wizard:**

1. Open the desired database.
2. On the Ribbon, select the **Create** tab.
3. On the **Create** tab, in the **Queries** group, click **Query Wizard** to display the **New Query** dialog box.
4. In the **New Query** dialog box, in the list box, select **Simple Query Wizard** and click **OK** to display the **Simple Query Wizard.**
5. In the **Simple Query Wizard,** on the **Which fields do you want in your query** page, from the **Tables/Queries** drop-down list, select a table or query to base your query on.
6. Add fields from the table or query to the **Selected Fields** list box.
    - In the **Available Fields** list box, select the desired fields and click the Add button or;
    - In the **Available Fields** list box, double-click the desired fields.
7. If necessary, in the **Simple Query Wizard,** on the **Which fields do you want in your query** page, from the **Tables/Queries** drop-down list, select another table or query that you want to add to your query and add fields from the table or query to the **Selected Fields** list box.
8. Click **Next.**
9. In the **Simple Query Wizard,** on the **Would you like a detail or summary query** page, select the desired option and click **Next.**
10. In the **What title do you want for your query** text box, enter a name for the query object.
11. Click **Finish** to close the wizard and to execute the query.
12. If necessary, close the database.

Procedure Reference: Create a Select Query Using the Query Design Feature

To create a select query using the Query Design feature:

1. Open the desired database.

2. On the Ribbon, select the **Create** tab.

3. On the **Create** tab, in the **Queries** group, click **Query Design** to open the **Show Table** dialog box.

4. Add tables and queries to the query by using the **Show Table** dialog box.

    a. In the **Show Table** dialog box, select a tab from which tables and queries can be added.

    ●   Select the **Tables** tab to display a list of tables in the database.

    ●   Select the **Queries** tab to display a list of queries in the database.

    ●   Select the **Both** tab to display a consolidated list of both the tables and queries in the database.

    b. Add a table or query to Design view

    ●   On the displayed tab, select the desired table or query, and click **Add** or;

    ●   On the displayed tab, double-click the desired table or query.

    c. If necessary, add more tables and queries to the Design view.

    d. Click **Close** to close the dialog box.

5. Add fields to the query design grid.

    ●   In a table or query field list, double-click the desired fields or;

    ●   In a table or query field list, drag the desired fields to the **Field** row of the query design grid.

6. Save the query.

    a. Display the **Save As** dialog box.

    ●   On the Quick Access toolbar, click the **Save** button or;

    ●   Select the **File** tab and choose **Save.**

    b. In the **Save As** dialog box, in the **Query Name** text box, type a name for the query.

    c. Click **OK.**

7. Run the query.

    ●   On the **Design** contextual tab, in the **Results** group, click **Run** or;

    ●   In the Navigation Pane, double-click the query to run it.

8. If necessary, save and close the database.

The Access Options Dialog Box

The **Access Options** dialog box provides you with various options to customize and configure the installation of the Access application. It provides options to customize the Ribbon and the Quick Access toolbar. It also provides various other customization options under various tabs such as **General, Current Database, Datasheet, Object Designers, Proofing, Language, Client Settings, Add-ins,** and **Trust Center.**

Trust Center

Access 2010 does not allow a query to be executed if a database is not placed in a trusted location. To enable the **Trust Center** settings:

1. In the **Access Options** dialog box, in the **Trust Center** category, click **Trust Center Settings.**

2. In the **Trust Center** dialog box, in the **Trusted Locations** category, click **Add New Location.**

3. In the **Microsoft Office Trusted Location** dialog box, specify the desired location.

4. If necessary, check the **Subfolders of this location are also trusted** check box and then click **OK.**

5. In the **Trust Center** dialog box, click **OK.**

6. In the **Access Options** dialog box, click **OK.**

ACTIVITY 4-1

Creating a Select Query by Using the Simple Query Wizard

Data Files:

C:\084306Data\Querying a Database\OGC Retail.accdb

Scenario:

You want to view and retrieve records of the weekly hours the employees put in along with their hourly pay. The relevant tables include more fields than is actually required for your current need. So, you decide to create a query that will display just the fields that you require.

---

1. Launch the **Simple Query Wizard** and add fields from the tblEmployees table to the query.

   a. On the **File** tab, click **Open.**

   b. Navigate to the C:\084306Data\Querying a Database folder and open the OGC Retail.accdb file.

   c. Select the **Create** tab, and in the **Queries** group, click **Query Wizard.**

   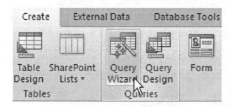

   d. In the **New Query** dialog box, verify that **Simple Query Wizard** is selected and click **OK.**

   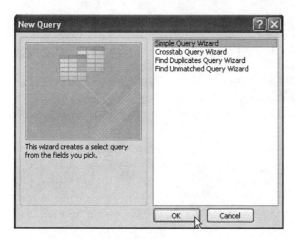

   e. In the **Simple Query Wizard,** on the **Which fields do you want in your query** page, from the **Tables/Queries** drop-down list, select **Table: tblEmployees.**

f.   In the **Available Fields** list box, double-click **LastName** to add the LastName field to the **Selected Fields** list box.

g.   Similarly, add the FirstName field to the **Selected Fields** list box.

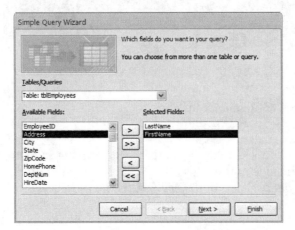

2.   Add the fields from the tblDepartments and tblHoursAndRates tables to the query design grid.

a.   On the **Which fields do you want in your query** page, from the **Tables/Queries** drop-down list, select **Table: tblDepartments.**

b.   In the **Available Fields** list box, double-click **DeptName** to add it to the **Selected Fields** list box.

c.   From the **Tables/Queries** drop-down list, select **Table: tblHoursAndRates.**

d.   In the **Available Fields** list box, double-click **WeeklyHours** and **HourlyRate** to add them to the **Selected Fields** list box and click **Next.**

e.   On the **Would you like a detail or summary query** page, observe that the **Detail (shows every field of every record)** option is selected and click **Next.**

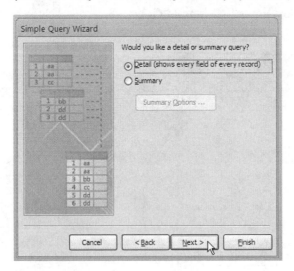

3.   Save the query.

a. In the **What title do you want for your query** text box, select the text "tblEmployees Query" and type *qryPayRates*

b. In the **Do you want to open the query or modify the query's design** section, observe that the **Open the query to view information** option is selected and click **Finish.**

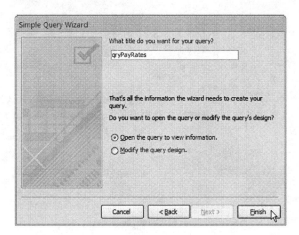

c. Observe that the results of the qryPayRates query are displayed in the document window.

d. Close the query.

ACTIVITY 4-2
Creating a Query by Using the Query Design Feature

Before You Begin:

The OGC Retail.accdb file is open.

Scenario:

You want to create a list with the details of the computers purchased in the organization. The required information is spread across two tables. You need to create a query to retrieve and display the required data.

---

1. Create a query.

   a. On the **Create** tab, in the **Queries** group, click **Query Design.**

   b. In the **Show Table** dialog box, on the **Tables** tab, select **tblInventory,** hold down **Ctrl** and select **tblPurchase,** and then click **Add.**

   c. Click **Close** to close the dialog box.

   d. Resize the field lists to display the complete field names.

   e. In the document window, in the tblInventory field list, double-click **Manufacturer** to add it to the query design grid.

   f. Similarly, from the tblPurchase field list, add the ManufacturerID, AssetTag, DateReceived, and PurchasePrice fields to the query design grid.

---

2. Run and save the query.

   a. On the **Design** contextual tab, in the **Results** group, click **Run** to run the query.

   b. Verify that the data for the fields added to the query is displayed.

   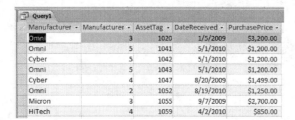

   c. On the Quick Access toolbar, click the **Save** button.

d. In the **Save As** dialog box, in the **Query Name** text box, type *qryInvoice* and click **OK.**

e. Observe that the qryInvoice query is displayed in the **Queries** section of the Navigation Pane.

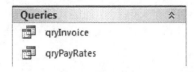

TOPIC B
Add Criteria to a Query

You used queries to retrieve data from multiple tables. Now, you are ready to retrieve data that satisfies specific conditions from one or more tables. In this topic, you will add criteria to a query.

You may need to locate all the records in a database with specific field values. By incorporating conditions into your query, you will be able to efficiently access this information. Displaying records by specifying such conditions in queries allows you to minimize the number of records you need to work with in large databases.

Query Criteria

Definition:

A *query criterion* is a search condition that is used in a query to retrieve or manipulate data selectively. Query criteria are used to retrieve data from records that meet the specified condition. More than one criterion can be included in a query. Query criteria are used to compare values in columns to a specific value. Calculations can also be performed on values in numeric columns before comparing information.

Example:

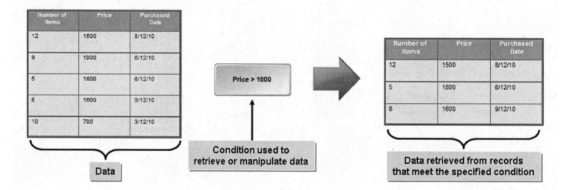

Figure 4-3: Criteria specified for a query.

Comparison Operators

Definition:

Comparison operators are operators that are used to compare two values. Comparison operators, when used in a query criterion, establish results after comparing two or more values. The output of a comparison operation is either true or false.

Example:

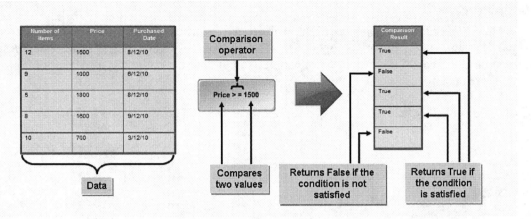

Figure 4-4: *The greater than or equal to comparison operator used as the criterion for comparing a column value.*

A List of Comparison Operators

Access supports the following comparison operators.

Operator	Description	Example	Result
=	Equal to	value1 = value2	Evaluates to true if value1 is equal to value2.
<	Less than	value1 < value2	Evaluates to true if value1 is less than value2.
<=	Less than or equal to	value1 <= value2	Evaluates to true if value1 is less than or equal to value2.
>	Greater than	value1 > value2	Evaluates to true if value1 is greater than value2.
>=	Greater than or equal to	value1 >= value2	Evaluates to true if value1 is greater than or equal to value2.
<>	Not equal to	value1 <> value2	Evaluates to true if value1 is not equal to value2.
Between And	Within a range	value1 Between value2 And value3	Evaluates to true if value1 is between value2 and value3.
Is Null	Null values	value1 Is Null	Evaluates to true if value1 is null.

Conditional Operators

Definition:

Conditional operators are operators that evaluate the result of one or more conditions. Conditional operators, like comparison operators, return a value of either true or false. Parentheses can be used to change the order of evaluation. Conditional operators are also referred to as logical operators.

Example:

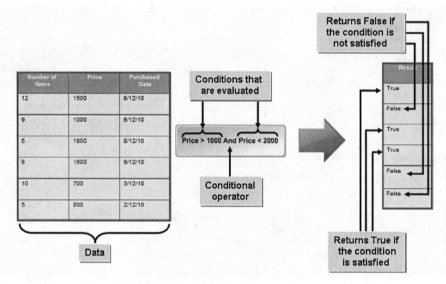

Figure 4-5: A conditional operator used to evaluate two conditions.

A List of Conditional Operators

Access supports the following conditional operators.

Operator	Value	Example	Result
AND	True if both conditions are true.	Condition1 AND Condition2	Evaluates to true if both Condition1 and Condition2 are true.
OR	True if either condition is true.	Condition1 OR Condition2	Evaluates to true if either Condition1 or Condition2 is true.
NOT	True if the condition is not true.	NOT Condition1	Evaluates to true if Condition1 is false.

Examples of Conditional Operators

The query design grid provides multiple rows in which you can identify records that need to be displayed in the result set. For example, if you want to select all the records where the value in the Price field is greater than $100, you would type *>100* in the **Criteria** row of the Price column. Using AND and OR would allow you to expand or narrow the search. If you want to select all the records where the value in the Price field is greater than $100 and where the location of the sale is the State of California, you would add the word *California* to the **Criteria** row of the State field column. Both criteria should be placed on the same line. This automatically creates an AND condition. An AND condition narrows the search, and the records that are selected must meet all the criteria in order to be returned.

Putting a criterion on a different line creates an OR condition, which expands the search. Using the previous example, if you were to move the word "California" one row below in the State field column, the query would return all the records where the Price field is greater than $100 as well as all records where the State field is equal to California only if there are no conditions in the criteria row of the other fields in the query design grid. If there are conditions in other fields, then the entire criteria row is evaluated as AND, and the row below is evaluated for OR, which may not give you the expected result. In such a scenario, you can type the second criterion in the same line of the criteria row as explained in the next paragraph.

AND and OR criteria may also be typed directly in the same cell of the criteria row. For example, you could type California or Michigan in a State criteria row, to return all records from either state. Typing California and Michigan in a State criterion row would return no records because the value in the State field cannot be equal to both.

How to Add Criteria to a Query

Procedure Reference: Add Criteria to a Query

To add criteria to a query:

1. Open the desired query.

2. Switch to the Design view.

3. If necessary, in the query design grid, include a field or fields for which you want to set criteria.

4. Include a criterion in the query.

   a. In the **Criteria** row for a field, type a comparison operator.

    You can avoid typing the "=" comparison operator when entering a criteria that needs to compare values or fields for equality. All other comparison operators must be entered.

   b. Type the value or field name that will be used to compare the field values.

5. If necessary, add more criteria to the query.

   • Include an **OR** condition in the same field.

      a. In the **or** row of the same field, type *OR*.

      b. Press the **Spacebar** and type another condition.

   • Include an **OR** condition in another field.

      a. In the **or** row of the desired field, type *OR*.

      b. Press the **Spacebar** and type another condition.

   • Include an **AND** condition in the same field.

      a. To the right of the included criteria, type *AND*.

      b. Press the **Spacebar** and type another condition.

   • In the **Criteria** row of the desired field, type a condition to include an **AND** condition in another field.

6. If necessary, add more criteria to the query with **AND** or **OR** conditional operators.

7. On the **Design** contextual tab, in the **Results** group, click **Run** to run the query.

ACTIVITY 4-3
Adding Criteria to a Query

Before You Begin:

The qryInvoice query in the OGC Retail.accdb file is open.

Scenario:

The Purchase department has solicited your help in finalizing the budget for purchase of new computers in the next financial year. They have requested crucial details needed to support their decision making. Specifically, they need information such as order details, computers purchased for a specific price from different manufacturers, and the oldest orders received between a specified date range. You suggest adding a query to locate the number of computers whose manufacturer details have not been updated.

---

1. Run the qryInvoice query to find the orders with a purchase price above $1000.

    a. In the Navigation Pane, double-click **qryInvoice** to run the query.

    b. Right-click the **qryInvoice** tab and choose **Design View.**

    c. In the query design grid, in the **Criteria** row of the PurchasePrice field, click and type *>1000*

    d. On the **Design** contextual tab, in the **Results** group, click **Run** to run the query.

    e. Observe that all 20 records displayed have a value in the PurchasePrice field that is greater than $1000.

    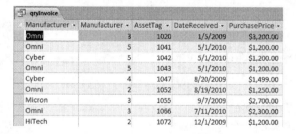

---

2. Add a criterion to the query to display records for computers purchased from a specific manufacturer.

    a. Right-click the **qryInvoice** tab and choose **Design View.**

b. In the query design grid, in the **Criteria** row for the Manufacturer field, click and type *Cyber*

c. On the **Design** contextual tab, in the **Results** group, click **Run** to run the query.

d. Observe that six records with Cyber as the manufacturer and a value in the PurchasePrice field that is greater than $1000 are displayed.

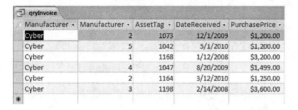

3. Add a criterion using the **or** operator to broaden the query to include another manufacturer's name.

a. On the **Home** tab, in the **Views** group, click **View** to view the query in the Design view.

b. In the query design grid, in the **Criteria** row, click after "Cyber" and type *or Atlas*

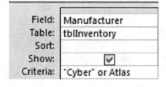

c. On the **Design** contextual tab, in the **Results** group, click **Run** to run the query.

d. Observe that the eight records displayed satisfy either of the conditions specified in the Manufacturer field and have a price greater than $1000.

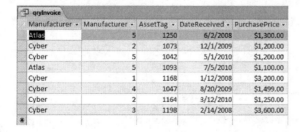

e. Switch to the Design view.

4. Add a criterion to determine the number of orders received during the first six months in 2008.

a.   In the query design grid, in the **Criteria** row for the DateReceived field, click and type *Between 1/1/2008 And 6/30/2008*

b.   Run the query.

c.   Observe that there are three records with values in the DateReceived field that fall between 1/1/2008 And 6/30/2008 and that they also satisfy all the conditions specified in the Manufacturer and Price fields.

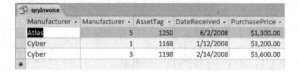

5.   Retrieve the records for orders received in the year 2010 and with purchase price above $1000.

    a.   Switch to the Design view.

    b.   In the query design grid, in the **Criteria** row for the DateReceived and Manufacturer fields, delete the criteria.

    c.   In the query design grid, in the **Criteria** row for the DateReceived field, type *>=1/1/2010*

    d.   Run the query.

    e.   Observe that there are seven records with orders received in the year 2010.

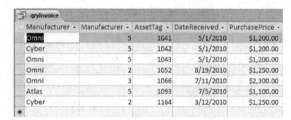

    f.   On the Quick Access toolbar, click the **Save** button and close the query.

TOPIC C
Add a Calculated Field to a Query

You added criteria to a query. Often, you may want to perform a calculation on values in fields and display these calculated values. In this topic, you will add a calculated field to a query.

Imagine that your company's payroll department wants you to calculate the weekly salary for employees who are paid by the hour. It certainly is not practical to manually calculate the salary for each employee. By including a calculated field that uses the employee's hourly rate, this is easily accomplished. Access allows you to calculate values based on fields and display them with the result of a query.

Calculated Fields

A *calculated field* is a field that displays values that are derived from calculations performed on values stored in other fields. Unlike other fields in a table, the values in a calculated field are not input by the user. The values of a calculated field will be calculated each time the query is run.

Arithmetic Operators

Definition:

Arithmetic operators are operators that are used to perform mathematical operations on values. Arithmetic operators require two operands to return the result of a mathematical calculation. These operators are commonly used to add, subtract, multiply, or divide values.

Example:

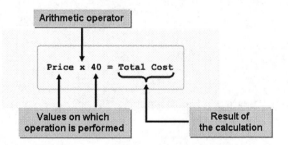

Figure 4-6: Arithmetic operators used to perform mathematical operations.

A List of Arithmetic Operators

Access provides a few commonly used arithmetic operators to perform calculations.

Arithmetic Operator	Description	Example	Result
+	Addition	value1 + value2	value1 is added to value2.
−	Subtraction	value1 − value2	value2 is subtracted from value1.

Arithmetic Operator	Description	Example	Result
*	Multiplication	value1 * value2	value1 is multiplied by value2.
/	Division	value1 / value2	value1 is divided by value2.

Expressions

Definition:

Expressions are combinations of functions, field names, numbers, text, and operators that allow you to perform calculations to produce results. An expression evaluates to a single value and is used to create calculated fields. You can use parentheses to group operations and expressions within another expression. When an operation or expression is within parentheses, it means that it is evaluated first and the result is used to evaluate the remainder of the expression. If there are nested sets of parentheses, then the innermost set is evaluated first.

Example:

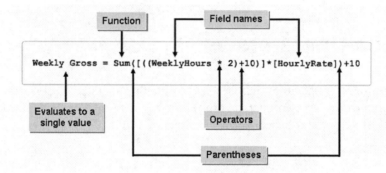

Figure 4-7: An expression to calculate the weekly gross pay.

The Expression Builder

The *Expression Builder* is a dialog box that allows you to select database objects and build expressions by using the application's built-in constants, operators, and functions. You can collapse or expand the **Expression Builder** to suit your needs.

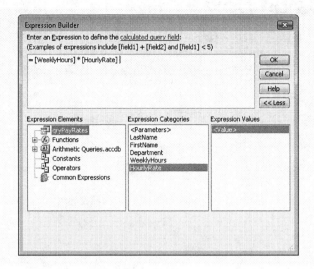

Figure 4-8: *The Expression Builder displaying options to build expressions.*

There are several components in the **Expression Builder** that allow you to create expressions.

Component	Function
The Expression text box	Displays the expression that is being built.
The **Expression Elements** list box	Displays queries, reports, common expressions, constants, and operators that can be added to the **Expression Values** list box.
The **Expression Categories** list box	Displays fields that are available in database tables that can be added to an expression.
The **Expression Values** list box	Displays constants and operators that can be added to the Expression text box to build an expression.

IntelliSense

The *IntelliSense* feature in Access 2010 allows you to effortlessly build expressions by automatically displaying the components of an expression that you might use in a given context, when you type the expression. When you build expressions by using the **Expression Builder** dialog box, the IntelliSense feature displays a drop-down list from which you can select the component you want to use in the expression. It also displays the complete component and a ScreenTip providing additional information about the item selected. The advantage of this feature is that it will help you minimize errors that may arise when working with long expressions and field names.

The Zoom Dialog Box

The *Zoom* dialog box enables you to type and view an entire expression. You can use the **Zoom** dialog box to view and edit an expression when it is too long to be displayed completely in the query design grid. To display an expression in the **Zoom** dialog box, right-click the field and choose **Zoom.**

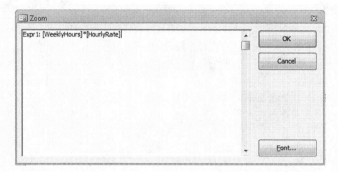

Figure 4-9: The Zoom dialog box displaying an expression for editing.

The Property Sheet Pane

The *Property Sheet* pane allows you to set properties for objects such as tables, queries, forms, and reports. It displays the properties of a selected field and allows you to specify the property values to define the structure, appearance, and behavior of the field. You can use the **Property Sheet** pane only in the Design view.

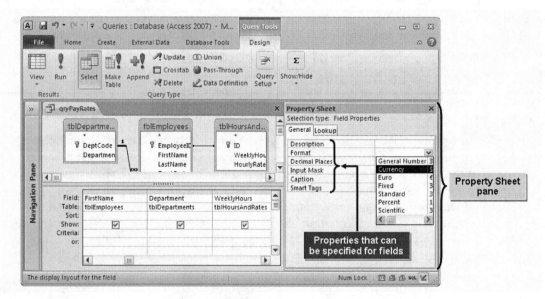

Figure 4-10: The Property Sheet pane displaying properties that can be set for a query.

How to Add a Calculated Field to a Query

Procedure Reference: Create an Expression in a Query

To create an expression in a query:

1. Open the desired query.
2. Switch to the Design view.
3. In the query design grid, right-click any available blank column and choose **Build** to display the **Expression Builder.**
4. In the **Expression Builder,** build the desired expression by adding the desired operators and field names.
   a. In the **Expression Elements** list box, select an element.
   b. In the **Expression Categories** list box, double-click a category to add it to the expression.
   c. In the **Expression Values** list box, double-click a value to include it in the expression.
   d. If necessary, add more operators, field names, or constants to complete the expression.
   e. Click **OK** to close the **Expression Builder.**
5. If necessary, change the name of the calculated field.
   a. Display the query in the Design view.
   b. Right-click the name of the calculated field and choose **Zoom.**
   c. In the **Zoom** dialog box, double-click the name of the calculated field and type the desired name.
   d. Click **OK** to close the **Zoom** dialog box.
6. Set the properties of the calculated field by using the **Property Sheet** pane.
   a. Select the calculated field, and on the **Design** contextual tab, in the **Show/Hide** group, click **Property Sheet** to display the **Property Sheet** pane.
   b. In the **Property Sheet** pane, click the blank field to the right of the desired property and type a value, or from the displayed drop-down list, select an appropriate value.
   c. Click the **Close** button to close the **Property Sheet** pane.
7. Click **Run** to run the query.
8. Save the query.
9. If necessary, save and close the database.

ACTIVITY 4-4
Adding a Calculated Field to a Query

Before You Begin:
The OGC Retail.accdb file is open.

Scenario:
You have a table in the database that stores details of employee work time and hourly wage. You are asked to calculate the weekly salaries for the employees in the company.

1. Create an arithmetic expression in the qryPayRates query.

    a. Open the qryPayRates query in the Design view.

    b. In the query design grid, right-click in the blank column after the HourlyRate column, and choose **Build** to open the **Expression Builder.**

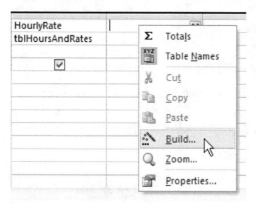

    c. In the **Expression Builder,** in the **Expression Elements** list box, select **Operators** to display the list of operators.

    d. In the **Expression Categories** list box, verify that **All** is selected.

    e. In the **Expression Values** list box, double-click the equal sign **(=)** to add it to the Expression text box.

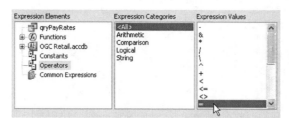

    f. In the **Expression Elements** list box, select **qryPayRates.**

    g. In the **Expression Categories** list box, double-click **WeeklyHours** to add it to the Expression text box and observe that it is enclosed in parentheses.

h. In the **Expression Elements** list box, select **Operators.**

i. In the **Expression Values** list box, double-click the multiplication sign (*) to add it to the Expression text box.

j. In the **Expression Elements** list box, select **qryPayRates.**

k. In the **Expression Categories** list box, double-click **HourlyRate** to add it to the expression.

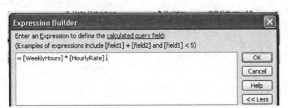

l. Click **OK** to close the **Expression Builder** dialog box.

2. Run the query and observe the results.

a. Run the query.

b. Observe that the values displayed in the last column are the product of the values in the WeeklyHours and HourlyRate fields.

WeeklyHour ▾	HourlyRate ▾	Expr1 ▾
40	$19.40	776
32	$21.00	672
35	$18.50	647.5
40	$20.00	800
40	$17.25	690
40	$23.50	940
40	$20.80	832

c. Switch to the Design view.

3. Change the name of the calculated field.

a. In the last column, right-click the calculated field and choose **Zoom.**

b. In the **Zoom** dialog box, in the text box, double-click **Expr1** and type *WeeklyGross*

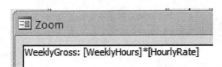

c. Click **OK** to close the **Zoom** dialog box.

d. Run the query.

e. Observe that the column header for the calculated field is now displayed as WeeklyGross.

WeeklyHour ▾	HourlyRate ▾	WeeklyGros ▾
40	$19.40	776
32	$21.00	672
35	$18.50	647.5
40	$20.00	800
40	$17.25	690
40	$23.50	940
40	$20.80	832

4. Display the values in the calculated field in the currency format.

a. Switch to the Design view. On the **Design** contextual tab, in the **Show/Hide** group, click **Property Sheet.**

b. In the **Property Sheet** pane, on the **General** tab, click the **Format** property, and from the drop-down list, select **Currency.**

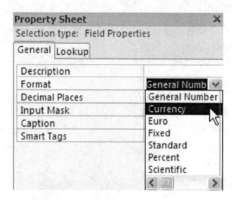

c. Click the **Close** button to close the **Property Sheet** pane, and run the query.

d. Observe that the values in the WeeklyGross field are now displayed with a dollar symbol and up to two decimals.

WeeklyHour ▾	HourlyRate ▾	WeeklyGros ▾
40	$19.40	$776.00
32	$21.00	$672.00
35	$18.50	$647.50
40	$20.00	$800.00
40	$17.25	$690.00
40	$23.50	$940.00
40	$20.80	$832.00

e. Save the query.

TOPIC D

Perform Calculations on a Record Grouping

You used a query to perform calculations on the field values of a record. You can also perform a calculation based on the values from a field in a set of records. In this topic, you will create a query that performs a calculation on a group of records.

One common job requirement for database users in a company is calculating payroll information. Developing a query that groups employees by department and then performing a calculation based on a field for the entire department may be a frequently required task. Access has features that allow you to group such data and perform calculations on them.

Group By Functions

Group By functions are functions that can be added to a query to perform calculations on values in a field from a group of records. They can be used to calculate a single value from values stored in a field of any number of records. The most commonly used functions calculate the sum, average, and count of values in a field, and the maximum and minimum values in a field. These functions can be specified in the Total row of the query design grid.

How to Perform Calculations on a Record Grouping

Procedure Reference: Perform Calculations on a Group of Records

To perform a calculation on a group of records:

1. Open the desired query in the Design view.
2. Enter the necessary criteria to group the records you want to view.
3. If necessary, display the **Total** row.
    *   Right-click in the query design grid and choose **Totals** or;
    *   On the **Design** contextual tab, in the **Show/Hide** group, click **Totals.**
4. Click in the **Total** row for the field you want to add values, and from the displayed drop-down list, select the desired option.
5. Run the query.
6. If necessary, save and close the database.

Procedure Reference: Remove Tables from a Query Window

To remove tables from a query window:

1. Open a query in the Design view.
2. In the query design window, select a table field list.
    *   On the **Home** tab, in the **Records** group, click **Delete** or;
    *   Right-click a table field list and choose **Remove Table.**

Procedure Reference: Remove Fields from the Query Design Grid

To remove fields from the query design grid:

1. Open a query in the Design view.
2. In the query design grid, select the desired column.
3. Delete the column.
   - On the **Design** contextual tab, in the **Query Setup** group, click **Delete Columns** or;
   - On the **Home** tab, in the **Records** group, click **Delete.**

Procedure Reference: Rearrange Fields in the Query Design Grid

To rearrange fields in the query design grid:

1. Open a query in the Design view.
2. Select a column.
3. Click and drag the column to the desired location in the query design grid.

Procedure Reference: Sort Records in the Query Design Grid

To sort records in the query design grid:

1. Open a query in the Design view.
2. In the query design grid, click in the desired column of the **Sort** row, and from the displayed drop-down list, select an option to specify the sort order.
   - Select **Ascending** to sort the query results in ascending order of the values in the column.
   - Select **Descending** to sort the query results in descending order of the values in the column.

Procedure Reference: Hide or Unhide Fields in the Query Results

To hide or unhide fields in the query results:

1. Open a query in the Design view.
2. In the query design grid, in the **Show** row, uncheck the check box for the fields to hide them in the query result.
3. If necessary, in the query design grid, in the **Show** row, check the check box for the fields to display them in the query result.

Options in the Total Row

By selecting the various options in the **Total** row, you can display the calculated results in a query as required.

- Select **Group By** to group the records based on similar values in a field.
- Select **Sum** to display the sum of values in a field.
- Select **Avg** to display the average of values in a field.
- Select **Min** to display the lowest value among all the values ina field.
- Select **Max** to display the highest value among all the values in a field.
- Select **Count** to display the number of values in a field.
- Select **StDev** to display the standard deviation of the values in a field.
- Select **Var** to display the variance of the values in a field.
- Select **First** to display the first value in a field.

- Select **Last** to display the last value in a field.
- Select **Expression** to allow you to perform calculations on the fields.
- Select **Where,** and in the **Criteria** row of the field, enter a condition to group records that satisfy this condition.

ACTIVITY 4-5
Performing a Calculation on a Group of Records

Before You Begin:

The qryPayRates query in the OGC Retail.accdb file is open.

Scenario:

The finance manager of your company has asked you for details on the number of hours worked and the wages paid to employees. He has asked you to provide the information for employees in each department in the company.

---

1. In the qryPayRates query, add the **Total** row to the query design grid.

   a. In the query design grid, observe that the **Total** row is not displayed.

   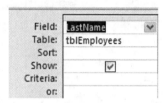

   b. On the **Design** contextual tab, in the **Show/Hide** group, click **Totals**.

   c. Observe that the **Total** row is added to the query design grid and the **Group By** function is displayed in the **Total** row for all fields.

   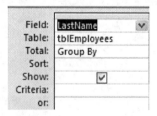

---

2. Group the records by the DeptName field.

   a. Run the query.

b. Observe that in the DeptName column, the department names do not appear in order and only the LastName column appears in order because the **Group By** function groups records from left to right.

c. Switch to the Design view.

d. In the query design grid, place the mouse pointer just above the first row of the DeptName column, and when the mouse pointer changes to a downward-pointing arrow, click to select the column.

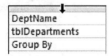

e. Click and drag the DeptName column to before the LastName column.

f. Run the query.

g. Observe that the DeptName column is grouped by department names because this is the first column now from left to right.

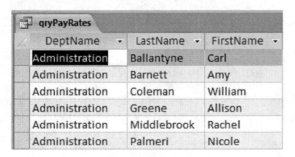

3. Remove the LastName, FirstName, and HourlyRate columns from the query design grid.

a. Switch to the Design view.

b. In the query design grid, place the mouse pointer just above the first row of the LastName column, and when the mouse pointer changes to a downward-pointing arrow, click to select the column.

c. Press **Delete** to delete the LastName column.

d. Similarly, select and delete the FirstName and HourlyRate columns.

e. Run the query.

f. Observe that the LastName, FirstName, and HourlyRate columns are deleted.

4. Calculate the average weekly hours and weekly payroll for each department.

    a. Switch to the Design view.

    b. Click in the **Total** row for the WeeklyHours field, and from the displayed drop-down list, select **Avg.**

    c. Click in the **Total** row for the WeeklyGross field, and from the displayed drop-down list, select **Sum.**

    d. Run the query.

    e. Observe that in the AvgOfWeek column, some of the values are displayed as a series of # symbols, because they have a long string of decimal values, making them too long to fit in the column.

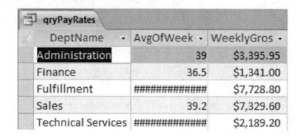

5. Modify the format of the WeeklyHours field.

    a. Switch to the Design view.

    b. Click in the WeeklyHours field, and on the **Design** contextual tab, in the **Show/Hide** group, click **Property Sheet** to display the **Property Sheet** pane.

    c. In the **Property Sheet** pane, on the **General** tab, click **Format,** and from the drop-down list, select **Fixed.**

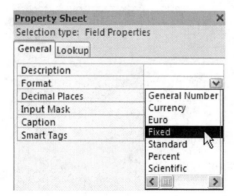

d.   In the **Property Sheet** pane, click **Decimal Places,** and from the drop-down list, select **2.**

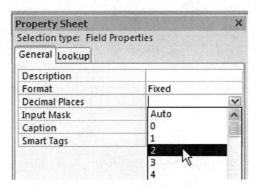

e.   Close the **Property Sheet** pane.

6.   Run and save the query.

a.   Run the query.

b.   Observe that the average hours worked by employees in a week in each department is displayed along with the weekly gross salary.

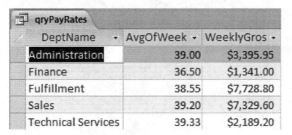

c.   Save and close the query.

d.   Close the database.

Lesson 4 Follow-up

In this lesson, you created queries. Your proficiency in querying a database for useful and selective information will allow you to efficiently retrieve the desired information from a table or from multiple tables and will greatly reduce the time it takes to present meaningful information based on data from a table.

1. **Which query object view will you use the most often while working with queries? Why?**

2. **Which type of operator do you think will be the most useful when working with queries? Why?**

5 | Designing Forms

Lesson Time: 30 minutes

Lesson Objectives:

In this lesson, you will design forms.

You will:

- Create a form.
- Modify the design of a form.
- View and edit data using an Access form.

Introduction

You used queries to retrieve information from a database. You may now want to view and manipulate data using a customized user interface. In this lesson, you will design forms to enter, edit, or delete data in a table.

When you open a database table in its default format, your monitor's screen is filled with rows and columns of entries. With such large amounts of data, searching for individual records not only consumes time, but also increases the chances of you committing errors and misinterpreting data. Creating a customized interface to add, view, and edit data one record at a time will expedite your work and reduce the chance of error.

TOPIC A
Create a Form

You executed queries to retrieve data from a table. Now, you may want to create forms that can be used to efficiently display the retrieved data and to enter and edit data in tables. In this topic, you will create a form using the form design tools available in Access.

After designing tables and populating them with data, users may need to include new records, edit existing data, view data in a certain format, or restrict access to certain fields in the table. You can do all these and more using forms.

Form Views

Access allows database users to view forms during form design, at runtime, or a combination of both.

View	Description
Form	A dynamic view that allows you to view data from a table or query on which the form is based. You can use this view to add and edit records, or navigate through the data. You will not be able to modify the design of the form in this view.
Design	A static view that helps you design a form. The Design view allows you to add a wide variety of form elements to a form. The properties of a form can be edited by using this view.
Layout	An interactive and dynamic view that you can use to create a form. It combines the features of the Form and Design views. You will be able to view data from tables as in the Form view. You can also make changes to the properties of the form elements, such as resizing and rearranging them, as in the Design view.

Form Sections

The Design view of a form consists of three sections: the Header section at the top displays information such as the form title; the Detail section in the middle displays the table records; and the Footer section at the bottom of the form displays additional information such as the current date and page number.

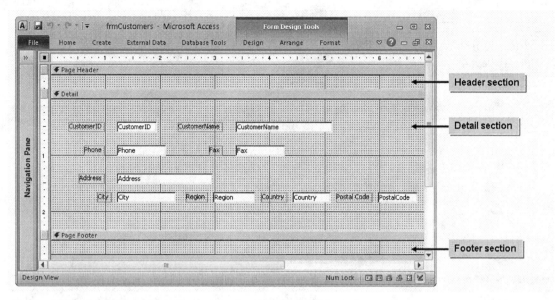

Figure 5-1: *The different sections of a form in the Design view.*

Form Creation Tools

Access includes a host of form creation tools that can be used interchangeably.

Form Creation Tool	Allows You To
Form	Create a form using all the fields in a table. If the table has a one-to-many relationship with another table, the form consists of a subform that is dependent on the related table. If the table has a one-to-many relationship with more than one table, the subform will not be created.
Form Design	Create a form in the Design view.
Blank Form	Create a blank form to which you can add the desired fields from a table or query.
Form Wizard	Create a form by selecting tables or queries and specifying fields to be included in a form.

Application Parts

Application parts are built-in Access templates that can be added to a database. Access provides you with various form layouts as application parts. These blank forms can be added to a database and modified to suit your requirements. The blank forms have a defined layout with placeholders for fields, which can be replaced with fields from any table. The **Application Parts** drop-down list is found in the **Templates** group on the **Create** tab.

Quick Start Applications

Application parts also provide templates for quickly creating databases for various purposes such as to maintain contacts, keep track of issues, consolidate tasks, maintain a user database, and store comments. These database templates contain forms along with tables, queries, and reports. When added to an existing database they can be linked to existing tables.

More Form Creation Options

The **More Forms** drop-down list provides access to more tools to create forms.

- **Multiple Items:** Generate a form that displays all the records in a table in the form of a spreadsheet.

- **Datasheet:** Create a form in the Datasheet view.

- **Split Form:** View a form simultaneously in the Form and Datasheet views. The Form view can be used to edit a record, while the Datasheet view can be used to navigate to a record.

- **Modal Dialog:** Create a modal form with the **OK** and **Cancel** buttons.

- **PivotChart:** Create a form in the PivotChart view.

- **PivotTable:** Create a form in the PivotTable view.

How to Create a Form

Procedure Reference: Create Forms Using the Form Creation Tools

To create forms using the various form creation tools:

1. Open an existing database that contains one or more tables.

2. Select a table for which you need to create a form.

3. On the **Create** tab, in the **Forms** group, select an option to generate a form.
    - Click **Form** to generate a simple form.
    - Click **Form Design** to generate a blank form in the Design view.
    - Click **Blank Form** to generate a blank form that can be customized.
    - Click **Form Wizard** to create a form by selecting tables or queries and specifying fields to be included in a form.
    - Click **More Forms** and select an option to create a form.

4. Once the form is generated, on the Quick Access toolbar, click **Save.**

5. In the **Save As** dialog box, in the **Form Name** text box, specify a name and click **OK.**

6. Close the database.

Procedure Reference: Create a Form Using the Form Wizard

To create a form using the **Form Wizard:**

1. Open an existing database that contains one or more tables and queries.

2. On the **Create** tab, in the **Forms** group, click **Form Wizard** to display the wizard.

3. On the first page of the **Form Wizard,** from the **Tables/Queries** drop-down list, select the desired table or query whose fields will be displayed in the **Available Fields** list box.

4. Move the desired fields from the **Available Fields** list box to the **Selected Fields** list box.

5. If necessary, add fields from other tables or queries and click **Next.**

6. On the **What layout would you like for your form** page, select the desired layout in which the form is to be displayed.

7. On the final page of the **Form Wizard,** in the text box, specify a name for the form.

8. Specify the option to open the form after it is created.

    ●   Select the **Open the form to view or enter information** option to open the form in the Form view.

    ●   Select the **Modify the form's design** option to open the form in the Design view.

9. Click **Finish.**

ACTIVITY 5-1
Creating a Form from a Table

Data Files:

C:\084306Data\Designing Forms\OGC Retail.accdb

Scenario:

While maintaining the employee database of your company, you realize that updating the database tables directly is time consuming. To facilitate the process, you decide to simplify the task of data entry and editing by creating a form. You want to try creating forms using the different options that Access provides to know its advantages.

1. Create a form using the **Form** tool and save the form.

    a. On the **File** tab, choose **Open.**

    b. In the **Open** dialog box, navigate to the C:\084306Data\Designing Forms folder and open the OGC Retail.accdb file.

    c. In the Navigation Pane, in the **Tables** section, select the **tblInventory** table.

    d. Select the **Create** tab, and in the **Forms** group, click **Form.**

    e. Observe that a form is created based on the fields in the tblInventory table.

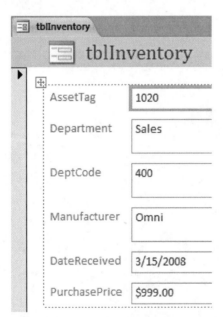

    f. On the Quick Access toolbar, click the **Save** button to save the form.

    g. In the **Save As** dialog box, in the **Form Name** text box, type *frmInventory* and click **OK.**

h.   Close the frmInventory form.

2.   Create a form using the **Form Wizard.**

    a.   Select the **Create** tab, in the **Forms** group, click **Form Wizard** to display the **Form Wizard.**

    b.   From the **Tables/Queries** drop-down list, select **Table: tblCustomers** to display all the fields of the tblCustomers table in the **Available Fields** list box.

    c.   Click the Add All button, [>>] to add all the fields of the table that are displayed in the **Available Fields** list box to the **Selected Fields** list box.

    d.   Observe that in the **Selected Fields** list box, the Quantity field is selected and click the Remove button, [<] to exclude it from the form.

    e.   Click **Next** to proceed to the next page of the wizard.

    f.   On the **What layout would you like for your form** page, observe that **Columnar** is selected and click **Next.**

    g.   On the **What title do you want for your form** page, in the text box, double-click **tblCustomers** and type *frmCustomers*

    h.   Observe that the **Open the form to view or enter information** option is selected and click **Finish.**

    i.   Observe that the form created using the wizard is open in the Form view.

    j.   Close the form.

TOPIC B
Modify the Design of a Form

You created forms using the form creation tools in Access. After creating a form, you may need to customize its design to suit your needs. In this topic, you will modify the design of a form.

In order to simplify the task of data entry, you may want to restructure the logical flow of information in a form and not follow the same sequence in which fields are present in the table. By rearranging form elements, you can make changes to forms to simplify data entry.

Controls

Definition:

A *control* is an object placed on the user interface of an application that allows a user to interact with the application. Controls are used to display data, obtain user input, perform an action, or enhance the user interface. Controls are commonly used in forms and reports. Controls can be selected, sized, aligned, and moved. They are generally labeled with context-significant names so that users can identify their purpose.

Example:

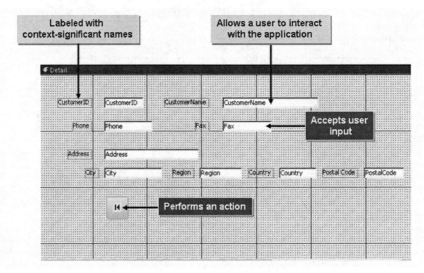

Figure 5-2: A form with various controls.

Types of Controls

Controls placed on a form can be broadly classified into three types, depending on the type of data they are associated with.

Control Type	Description
Bound	A control that is associated with data from a field in a table or query. You can use bound controls to retrieve and display data from a table or query. The data displayed by a bound control can be of any type, including text, numbers, boolean values, or images.
Unbound	A control that is not necessarily static. It can have calculated values and other dynamic user defined content in the control. Unbound controls are not linked to a table or query.
Calculated	A control that displays data obtained by evaluating an arithmetic expression. An arithmetic expression can use data from another control in the form, or it can retrieve values from a field in the form's underlying table or query.

Grouped Controls

Grouped controls are two or more controls that can be treated as one unit while designing a form or report. You can select a group instead of selecting each individual control while arranging controls or assigning properties. When you group controls, a colored box appears around all of the selected objects.

Form Layouts

A *form layout* is the design and arrangement of various controls, such as text boxes and labels on a form. Access offers form layout tools that help you format and arrange the controls on a form in the specified layout. There are two types of layouts; the **Tabular** layouts that display controls horizontally and the **Stacked** layouts that display controls vertically. The **Control Padding** property is used to set the space between the gridline and the control. The **Control Margins** property is used to decide the location of values within a control.

The Property Sheet Pane

The **Property Sheet** pane displays the properties that you can set for the controls on a form. You can set properties for controls such as text boxes, images, labels, or combo boxes. You can access the **Property Sheet** pane from the **Tools** group on the **Design** contextual tab. The properties in the **Property Sheet** pane are grouped into five functional tabs.

Tab	Function
Format	Sets properties for the font, color, line spacing, and text alignment.
Data	Sets properties for data validation, format, and the input mask.
Event	Sets properties for mouse and key press events.
Other	Sets other advanced properties.
All	Sets all properties of a control.

The WYSIWYG Interface

The *What You See Is What You Get (WYSIWYG)* interface enables you to modify the layouts of a form when you are working in the Layout view. You do not need to go either into the Design view to modify the layout or to the Form view to view how the form will appear. This reduces the time and effort you spend while designing and formatting a form.

The Anchoring Tool

The *anchoring tool* is used to position the controls in the form layout. Anchoring enables you to position and resize a control within a form. There are various anchoring options available, such as **Top Left, Stretch Down,** and **Bottom Left.**

Anchoring Options

The anchoring options determine how controls are positioned in a form layout.

Option	*Positions the Controls*
Top Left	At the top-left corner of the form layout.
Stretch Across Top	Stretched across the top of the form layout.
Top Right	At the top-right corner of the form layout.
Stretch Down	On the left side of the form layout vertically.
Stretch Down and Across	By spreading across the form layout.
Stretch Down and Right	On the right side of the form layout vertically.
Bottom Left	At the bottom-left corner of the form layout.
Stretch Across Bottom	Stretched across the bottom of the form layout.
Bottom Right	At the bottom-right corner of the form layout.

The Tab Order

Tab order is the logical flow of information on a form as indicated by the use of the **Tab** key. Selecting a control in a form and then pressing **Tab** will move the focus to the next control that is in line with the flow of information on the form. By default, the tab order is left to right within each row of controls.

The Tab Order in Forms

When you create a form using a **Form Wizard,** Access sets the tab order from top to bottom or from left to right. When you create a form using the **Form Design** tool, the tab order that is created by default can be modified to match any change in the way tab controls are displayed on the form.

How to Modify the Design of a Form

Procedure Reference: Modify a Form

To modify a form:

1. Open a form in the Design view.
2. If necessary, move the controls.
   - Move just the text box or label and not its associated component.
     a. Select the control.
     b. Click and drag the control to the desired position.
   - Move the text box or label with its associated component, or a group of controls.
     a. Select the controls.
     b. Move the mouse pointer anywhere on top of the control other than the upper-left corner until you see a four-headed arrow.
     c. Click and drag the controls to the desired position.
3. If necessary, resize the controls.
   - Drag a sizing handle to increase or decrease the size.
   - On the **Arrange** tab, in the **Sizing & Ordering** group, from the **Size/Space** drop-down list, select **To Fit.**
4. If necessary, align the controls.
   a. Select the controls you want to align.
   b. Right-click the selected controls and choose **Align** and then choose the appropriate alignment setting.
      - Choose **To Grid** to align the upper-left corners of the selected controls to the nearest point in the grid.
      - Choose **Left** to left-align the controls.
      - Choose **Right** to right-align the controls.
      - Choose **Top** to move the lower controls up and align their edges with the bottom edge of the previous control.
      - Choose **Bottom** to move the upper controls down and align their bottom edges with the top edge of the next control.
5. If necessary, adjust the tab order of the form fields.
   a. On the **Design** contextual tab, in the **Tools** group, click **Tab Order.**
   b. In the **Tab Order** dialog box, click **Auto Order** and click **OK.**
6. If necessary, use the **Design** contextual tab and apply formatting to text boxes or labels.
7. If necessary, on the **Design** contextual tab, in the **Header/Footer** group, click **Title** to add a title or other descriptive text.
8. If necessary, resize the form window to change the size of the form.
9. Save and close the form.

Procedure Reference: Format and Arrange the Controls on a Form

To format and arrange the controls on a form:

1. Open a form in the Layout view.
2. In the form, select the desired controls.

3. Design a form.

- On the **Format** contextual tab, in the **Selection, Font, Number, Background,** and **Control Formatting** groups, select the desired command and specify the setting to format the controls.

- On the **Arrange** contextual tab, in the **Table, Rows & Columns, Merge/Split, Move, Position,** and **Sizing & Ordering** groups, select the desired command and specify the settings to arrange the controls.

4. Position and format the controls.

- On the **Arrange** contextual tab, in the **Position** group, from the **Anchoring** drop-down list, select the desired option to anchor the controls.

- On the **Arrange** contextual tab, in the **Position** group, from the **Control Padding** drop-down list, select the desired option to space the controls.

- On the **Arrange** contextual tab, in the **Position** group, from the **Control Margins** drop-down list, select the desired option to margin the controls.

5. Save the form.

6. If necessary, switch to the Form view.

7. If necessary, view, insert, or update records.

8. If necessary, save and close the database.

Procedure Reference: Format Form Controls as a Table

To format form controls as a table:

1. Open a form in the Design view.

2. On the **Format** contextual tab, in the **Selection** group, click **Select All** to select all the controls in the form.

3. On the **Arrange** contextual tab, in the **Table** group, click **Tabular** to arrange the controls of the form in a tabular format.

4. If necessary, insert a row or column.

- Click **Insert Above** to insert a row above the selected control.

- Click **Insert Below** to insert a row below the selected control.

- Click **Insert Left** to insert a column to the left of the selected control.

- Click **Insert Right** to insert a column to the right of the selected control.

5. If necessary merge the controls.

a. Select two or more controls.

b. On the **Arrange** contextual tab, in the **Merge/Split** group, click **Merge** to merge the controls into a single control.

6. If necessary, split the controls.

- Click **Split Vertically** to split the control vertically.

- Click **Split Horizontally** to split the control vertically.

7. If necessary, move the controls up or down.

- Select the desired control, and on the **Arrange** contextual tab, in the **Move** group, click **Move Up** to move a control above a particular control.

- Select the desired control, and on the **Arrange** contextual tab, in the **Move** group, click **Move Down** to move a control below a particular control.

8. Save the form and switch to the Form view to view the changes.

Procedure Reference: Group the Form Controls

To group the form controls:

1. In the Design view of a form, select the controls that you want to group.
2. On the **Arrange** contextual tab, in the **Sizing & Ordering** group, from the **Size/Space** drop-down list, select **Group** to group the controls.
3. If necessary, perform the essential actions on the grouped controls.
4. If necessary, in the **Sizing & Ordering** group, from the **Size/Space** drop-down list, select **Ungroup** to ungroup the controls.

Procedure Reference: Add a Form Header and Footer

To add a form header and footer:

1. Open a form in the Design view.
2. On the **Design** contextual tab, in the **Header/Footer** group, click **Title** to display the form's header and footer.
3. If necessary, add essential controls to the form header and footer.
4. Format the header and footer.
    *   Replace the default title with the desired title.
    *   On the **Design** contextual tab, in the **Header/Footer** group, click **Logo,** and in the **Insert Picture** dialog box, navigate to the desired location, select a picture, and click **OK.**
    *   On the **Design** contextual tab, in the **Header/Footer** group, click **Date and Time,** and in the **Date and Time** dialog box, select the desired options and click **OK.**

Procedure Reference: Add an Image to a Form

To add an image to a form:

1. Open a form in the Design view.
2. On the **Design** contextual tab, in the **Controls** group, select the **Image** tool.
3. On the form, click where you want to display the image.
4. In the **Insert Picture** dialog box, navigate to the desired location, select the desired file, and click **OK.**
5. If necessary, display the **Property Sheet** pane and set the desired properties for the image control.
6. If necessary, resize and relocate the image on the form.

Procedure Reference: Add a Background Image to a Form

To add a background image to a form:

1. Open the form to which you want to add a background image in the Design view.
2. Select the **Format** contextual tab, and in the **Background** group, click **Background Image.**
    *   From the displayed gallery, select an image or;
    *   From the displayed gallery, select **Browse,** and in the **Insert Picture** dialog box, navigate to the desired location, select an image and click **OK.**

Procedure Reference: Apply Font Properties to Controls

To apply font properties to controls:

1. Display a form in the Design or Layout view.
2. Select a control.
3. On the **Format** contextual tab, in the **Font** group, specify the desired property.

ACTIVITY 5-2
Modifying a Form

Before you Begin:

The OGC Retail.accdb file is open.

Scenario:

As part of a new venture in your organization to improve user interfaces in applications, a coworker has modified the form that you had created using the **Form Design** tool to create a custom form that is more versatile and interactive. On further review, you realize that some of the controls can be rearranged to improve the appearance of the form.

1. Check the tab order of the form.

   a. In the Navigation Pane, in the **Forms** section, double-click **frmCustomers** to open it in the Form view.

   b. Press **Tab** eight times to move from the first field in the form to the last.

   c. Observe that the tab order moves sequentially one after another.

2. Rearrange the controls on the form.

   a. Switch to the Design view.

   b. Move the mouse pointer over the top edge of the **Form Footer** band and when the mouse pointer changes into a double-headed arrow, click and drag it down to the 3.5 inch mark on the vertical ruler.

   c. In the document window, in the **Detail** section, select the **Fax** label control, hold down **Shift,** and select the **Fax** text box control.

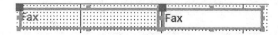

    d.   Drag the **Fax** label and text box controls to place them below the **Phone** label and text box controls.

    e.   Select the **Region** label control, hold down **Shift,** and select the **Region** text box control.

    f.   Drag the **Region** label and text box controls to place them above the **Country** label and text box controls.

3.   Switch to the Form view to check the tab order.

    a.   On the **Design** contextual tab, in the **Views** group, from the **View** drop-down list, select **Form View.**

    b.   Press **Tab** four times.

    c.   Observe that the Region field should logically follow the City field, but the tab order takes you to the Fax field.

    d.   Press **Tab** four times to move to the **Phone** field.

4.   Correct the tab order of the form.

    a.   Switch to the Design view.

    b.   On the **Design** contextual tab, in the **Tools** group, click **Tab Order.**

    c.   In the **Tab Order** dialog box, in the **Custom Order** list box, observe that the fields are listed in the order they appeared on the form.

    d.   Click **Auto Order** and then click **OK** to set the tab order to the order in which the fields are listed on the form.

5.   Return to the Form view and check the tab order.

    a.   Switch to the Form view.

    b.   Press **Tab** eight times to move through the fields.

    c.   Observe that the tab order is corrected to suit the form's new layout.

6.   Format the form.

    a.   Switch to the Design view.

    b.   Click outside the top-left corner of the CustomerID label control and drag to the bottom-right corner of the **Detail** section to select all the controls.

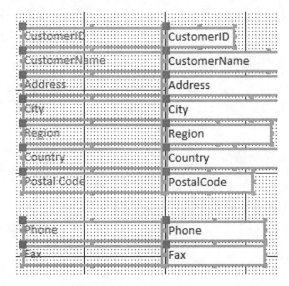

    c.   On the Ribbon, select the **Arrange** contextual tab.

    d.   On the **Arrange** contextual tab, in the **Table** group, click **Stacked.**

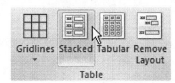

    e.   In the **Position** group, from the **Control Padding** drop-down list, select **Medium.**

    f.   Observe that the controls on the form are equally spaced out.

    g.   In the **Sizing & Ordering** group, from the **Align** drop-down list, select **Right** to align the form to the center of the work area.

7.   Add borders for the controls.

    a.   In the **Table** group, from the **Gridlines** drop-down list, select **Width** and then select **Hairline,** which is the first option.

    b.   From the **Gridlines** drop-down list, select **Border** and then select **Solid,** which is the second option.

c. From the **Gridlines** drop-down list, select **Color** and from the Colors gallery, in the **Standard Colors** section, in the last row, select **Dark Blue,** which is the second color from the right.

8. Check whether the controls are anchored to the top-left of the form.

   a. On the **Arrange** contextual tab, in the **Position** group, from the **Anchoring** drop-down gallery, verify that **Top Left** is selected.

   b. Click **Anchoring** again to hide the gallery.

   c. Switch to the Form view.

   d. Observe that the controls are anchored to top left in the form.

   e. Save the form.

TOPIC C

View and Edit Data Using an Access Form

You created a form using Access. Now, you may want to control the way the data from a table or query is presented to users. In this topic, you will view and edit data using forms.

When working with a database, you may need to view and update specific information frequently. Access allows you to view and navigate to different records quickly and efficiently using forms.

How to View and Edit Data Using an Access Form

Procedure Reference: Add Records to a Table Using a Form

To add records to a table using a form:

1. Open a form.
2. On the Record Navigation bar, click the **New (blank) record** button.
3. In the empty form that is displayed, enter the appropriate data.
4. When all desired fields are filled with data, close the form.
5. If necessary, open the table and verify that the new record is created.

Procedure Reference: View Records Using a Form

To view records using a form:

1. Open a database with forms.
2. Open a form in the Form view.
    *   In the Navigation Pane, right-click the desired form and choose **Open** or;
    *   In the Navigation Pane, double-click the desired form.
3. Navigate through the records using the Record Navigation bar.
    *   Click the **Next Record** button to display data from the succeeding record in the table.
    *   Click the **Previous Record** button to display data from the preceding record in the table.
    *   Click the **Last Record** button to display data from the last record of the table.
    *   Click the **First Record** button to display data from the first record of the table.
    *   In the **Current Record** text box, delete the current entry, enter a record number, and press **Enter** to display data for the corresponding record.
4. Close the database.

Procedure Reference: Search Records Based on a Criterion

To search records based on a criterion:

1. Open a database with forms that have been designed previously.
2. Open a form to display data from a table.
3. On the **Home** tab, in the **Find** group, click **Find.**

4. In the **Find and Replace** dialog box, in the **Find What** text box, type the text that needs to be searched for, and, if desired, set the **Look In, Match Values,** and other settings in the dialog box.

5. Click **Find Next** to display the first record that matches the search criteria in the form.

6. If necessary, click **Find Next** to display more records that match the search criteria in the form.

7. Close the database.

Procedure Reference: Filter Data in a Form

To filter data in a form:

1. Open a form and select the field to which the filter has to be applied.

2. On the **Home** tab, in the **Sort & Filter** group, click **Filter** and specify the desired filter settings.

3. If necessary, view, insert, or update records using the form.

4. If necessary, in the **Sort & Filter** group, click **Toggle Filter** to remove the filter.

Procedure Reference: Sort Data in a Form

To sort data in a form:

1. Open a form and select the field based on which sorting has to be applied.

2. On the **Home** tab, in the **Sort & Filter** group, select the desired sort option.

   - Select the **Ascending** option to sort the field in ascending order.

   - Select the **Descending** option to sort the field in descending order.

   - From the **Advanced** drop-down list, select **Advanced Filter/Sort** and specify the desired criteria.

Navigation in an Access Form

To move through the fields of a record displayed in a form, you can use the mouse or keys and keystroke combinations. Refer to the navigation methods in the following table.

Keystroke	*Allows You To*
Tab, Enter, Right Arrow, Down Arrow	Move to the next field in a record. If you are in the last field of a record, pressing any of these keys will transfer control to the first field of the next record.
Shift+Tab, Left Arrow, Up Arrow	Move to the previous field in a record. If you are in the first field in a form, pressing any of these keys will transfer control to the last field of the previous record.
Page Up	Move to the same field in the previous record.
Page Down	Move to the same field in the next record.
Home	Move to the first field of the record you are currently in.
End	Move to the last field of the record you are currently in.
Ctrl+Home	Move to the first field in the first record of the table that you are working on.
Ctrl+End	Move to the last field in the last record of the table that you are working on.

ACTIVITY 5-3
Viewing Records Using an Access Form

Before You Begin:

The OGC Retail.accdb file is open.

Scenario:

The Sales department has standardized the collection of customer information. They have designed a new form for adding customer information in a table. Because you regularly work with data and know what kind of information can be stored in a database, they have asked you to review the form. You decide the best way to evaluate the form is to navigate through it to examine its functioning.

1. Navigate through the records in the frmCustomers form.

   a. On the Record Navigation bar, click the **Next record** button, [▶] twice to view the third record of the table.

   b. Click the **Previous record** button, [◀] to view the second record of the table.

   c. Click the **Last record** button, [▶|] to view the last record of the table.

   d. Click the **First record** button, [|◀] to view the first record of the table.

   e. In the **Current Record** text box, triple-click the text **1 of 14.**

   f. Type **4** and press **Enter** to view the fourth record of the table.

2. Search using a criterion.

   a. On the **Home** tab, in the **Find** group, click **Find.**

   b. In the **Find and Replace** dialog box, on the **Find** tab, in the **Find What** text box, type **supersaver**

   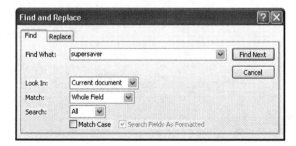

   c. In the **Look In** drop-down list, verify that **Current document** is selected.

   d. In the **Search** drop-down list, verify that **All** is selected and click **Find Next.**

   e. Observe that the form displays the information for the customer, SuperSaver.

       f.   Click the **Close** button to close the **Find and Replace** dialog box.

3.   Apply a filter to display only those records with country Canada.

       a.   In the displayed record, click in the **Country** text box control.

       b.   On the **Home** tab, in the **Sort & Filter** group, click **Filter.**

       c.   In the drop-down list, uncheck the **(Select All)** check box, check the **Canada** check box, and click **OK.**

       d.   Observe that only two records are displayed. On the Record Navigation bar, click the **Next Record** button to view the next record.

4.   Sort the records in descending order of customer IDs.

       a.   On the **Home** tab, in the **Sort & Filter** group, click **Toggle Filter.**

       b.   Observe that all the records are displayed.

       c.   On the **Home** tab, in the **Sort & Filter** group, select **Descending** to display the records in descending order.

       d.   On the Record Navigation bar, click the **Next Record** button four times and observe that the records are sorted in descending order of customer IDs.

       e.   Save the form and close the database.

Lesson 5 Follow-up

In this lesson, you designed forms. By effectively using the form design tools, you will be able to create esthetic forms that help users view and enter data easily.

1. **Under what circumstances will you modify the design of a form?**

2. **Which form-related features in Access do you expect to use often when designing a form?**

6 | Generating Reports

Lesson Time: 45 minutes

Lesson Objectives:

In this lesson, you will generate reports.

You will:

- Create a report.
- Add a control to a report.
- Format the controls in a report.
- Enhance the appearance of a report.
- Prepare a report for print.

Introduction

You created forms to view and manipulate data in records. However, when you need to make decisions based on this data, you will likely want to generate a report, which presents the data as meaningful information. In this lesson, you will use the Access report development and design tools to generate reports.

Assume that the total sales of your company's products has dropped in the current fiscal year. You may want to examine the reasons behind the declining product sales. Information on product sales is currently held in a large database, and viewing each of the records will not be of much help in your analysis. You can use the reporting feature of the database to summarize the total sales for each product, region, and salesperson. You can then make appropriate decisions based on these reports.

TOPIC A
Create a Report

You created forms to enter and edit data. Now, you may want to create reports for analyzing data that can be subsequently printed. In this topic, you will create a report.

A report has many advantages. A thoughtful design will organize raw data in ways that will make it far more meaningful. Report tools make it easy to generate summary statistics such as totals and averages that are of key importance to decision makers. Access offers you a variety of report creation tools to create effective reports with information that can be quickly grasped and absorbed by others.

Report Views

Access 2010 provides four views that can be used to create, edit, and view reports. The choice of which view to use depends on the task you need to perform.

View	Description
Report	A dynamic view that allows you to view data from a table or query on which the report is based. You can use this view to see only the data present in the table.
Print Preview	A view that is used to check how a report will look when printed. In this view, only the **Print Preview** tab is enabled. You can use the various options in the **Page Layout** group on the **Print Preview** tab to set the report page layout before printing the report.
Design	A view that provides you with a skeletal view of the structure of a report. You can add, modify, or delete controls such as labels and images in the Design view.
Layout	An interactive and dynamic view that you can use to create or modify a report. It is a combination of the Report and Design views. In this view, you can view the data bound to a control and make changes to the properties of the controls such as resizing and rearranging the controls as in the Design view.

Report Creation Tools

Reports can be created based on data in tables or from queries. Access 2010 includes a number of tools that help you create reports.

Tool	Used To
Report	Create a report that uses all the fields in a table or query. The report will be displayed in the Layout view.
Blank Report	Add fields from tables and queries to create a report by displaying a blank report with necessary options. The report will be displayed in the Layout view. You can create the report by adding and positioning controls according to your requirements.

Tool	Used To
Report Design	Create a new report or edit an existing one in the Design view. You can add fields from tables and queries. The report will be displayed in the Layout view.
Report Wizard	Create a report by adding fields from tables and queries. You can also group and sort the data in a report and customize the layout of a report.

The Report Wizard

The *Report Wizard* helps you create a report by following a step-by-step guided approach. Using the wizard is recommended when you are creating reports from more than one table or query. You can select the tables or queries and the fields from them that you want to include in the report. The wizard also provides options for grouping and sorting data, and for customizing the layouts of reports.

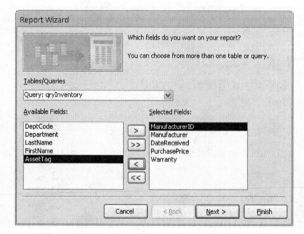

Figure 6-1: *The Report Wizard displaying options to select fields that are to be included in a report.*

Summary Options

When creating a report using the **Report Wizard,** Access allows you to summarize data. Using the **Summary Options** dialog box, you can choose functions such as sum, average, minimum, and maximum to be used on numeric fields in a table. There are also options to display all the records and the result returned by the aggregate function, or only the result returned by the aggregate function for a group of data. You can also set the option to calculate the percent of total for sums.

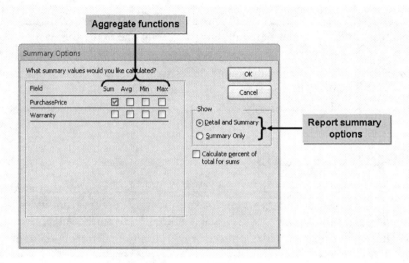

Figure 6-2: The Summary Options dialog box displaying options to summarize data in a report.

How to Create a Report

Procedure Reference: Create a Blank Report

To create a blank report:

1. On the **Create** tab, in the **Reports** group, click **Blank Report.**
2. Add the desired controls and content to the report.
3. Save the report.
    a. On the Quick Access toolbar, click **Save.**
    b. In the **Save As** dialog box, in the **Report Name** text box, type the desired name.
    c. Click **OK** to save the report.

Procedure Reference: Create a Report Based on the Data in a Table

To create a report based on the data in a table:

1. In the Navigation Pane, select the desired table.
2. On the **Create** tab, in the **Reports** group, click **Report.**
3. Save the report with the desired name.

Procedure Reference: Create a Report Using the Report Wizard

To create a report using the **Report Wizard:**

1. Open an existing Access database.
2. Select the **Create** tab.
3. In the **Reports** group, click **Report Wizard.**
4. In the **Report Wizard,** on the **Which fields do you want on your report** page, from the **Tables/Queries** drop-down list, select the required table or query.
5. In the **Available Fields** list box, double-click the required fields to add them to the **Selected Fields** list box.
6. If necessary, select fields from other tables or queries and click **Next.**

7. In the **Report Wizard,** in the **Do you want to add any grouping levels** list box, double-click a field to group the records based on that field and click **Next.**

8. On the **What sort order do you want for detail records** page, from the **You can sort records by up to four fields, in either ascending or descending order** drop-down list, select a field.

9. Toggle the button between **Ascending** and **Descending** to set the sort order for the field.

10. If necessary, select other fields and set the sort order for them.

11. If necessary, set options to summarize the values in a report.

    a. Click the **Summary Options** button to open the **Summary Options** dialog box.

    b. In the **Summary Options** dialog box, for the desired fields, check the check boxes for the aggregate function to summarize the values in the field.

    c. In the **Show** section, select the desired option for displaying a detailed summary or only the summary.

    d. If necessary, check the **Calculate percent for total of sums** check box and click **OK.**

12. Click **Next.**

13. On the **How would you like to lay out your report** page, select the required layout for the report and click **Next.**

14. In the **What title do you want for your report** text box, type a name for the report and click **Finish.**

15. If necessary, close the report and the database.

ACTIVITY 6-1
Creating a Report

Data Files:

C:\084306Data\Generating Reports\OGC Retail.accdb

Scenario:

Your manager has invited you for a meeting to discuss the hardware inventory of the company. To prepare yourself for the meeting, you need to create a report with important details on the allocation of computers.

1. Generate a report to add all the fields from a table.

    a. On the **File** tab, click **Open.**

    b. Navigate to the C:\084306Data\Generating Reports folder and open the OGC Retail.accdb file.

    c. In the Navigation Pane, select **tblInventory.**

    d. Select the **Create** tab, and in the **Reports** group, click **Report.**

    e. Observe that a report containing the data in the tblInventory table is generated.

    f. On the Quick Access toolbar, click **Save.**

    g. In the **Save As** dialog box, in the **Report Name** text box, type *rptInventory* and click **OK.**

    h. Close the rptInventory report.

2. Generate a report by selecting the required fields from a table.

    a. Select the **Create** tab, and in the **Reports** group, click **Report Wizard.**

b. In the **Report Wizard,** on the **Which fields do you want on your report** page, from the **Tables/Queries** drop-down list, select **Table: tblPurchase.**

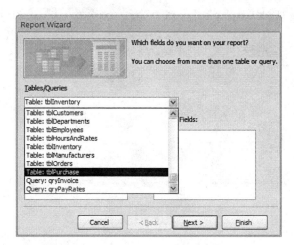

c. Observe that the fields in the tblPurchase table are displayed in the **Available Fields** list box.

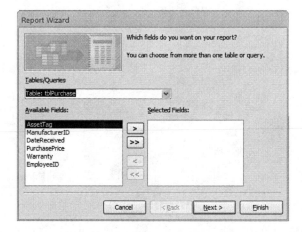

d. In the **Available Fields** list box, double-click the **AssetTag, ManufacturerID, DateReceived,** and **PurchasePrice** fields to add them to the **Selected Fields** list box and click **Next.**

e. On the **Do you want to add any grouping levels** page, click **Next.**

f. On the **What sort order do you want for your records** page, click **Next.**

g. On the **How would you like to lay out your report** page, in the **Layout** section, verify that **Tabular** is selected, and in the **Orientation** section, verify that **Portrait** is selected and click **Next.**

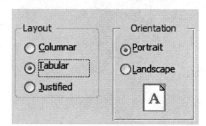

h.   In the **What title do you want for your report** text box, double-click the default name and type *rptPurchase* and click **Finish.**

i.   Observe that all the selected fields are displayed in the report and close the report.

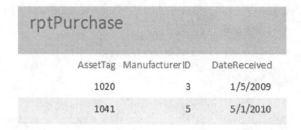

TOPIC B
Add a Control to a Report

You generated reports using different creation tools. However, there might be instances where you need to display additional fields in the report. In this topic, you will add controls to a report.

You may need to perform calculations on values from table fields and display the values in a report. One such instance may be during the holiday season when commercial establishments come up with various promotional offers and sell products at discounted prices. A new price list will need to be generated based on the original prices. Using Access, you can accomplish this by adding a control, which displays the final product price after the discount.

Report Sections

The Design view of a report consists of a header and footer band for the report, page, and group sections. While information that needs to appear on every page of a printed report is entered in the page header and footer, information that needs to appear for each group of data is entered in the group header and footer. Information that needs to appear only once, at the beginning or at the end of a report, is entered in the report header and footer, respectively.

The **Detail** section in the middle displays the table records.

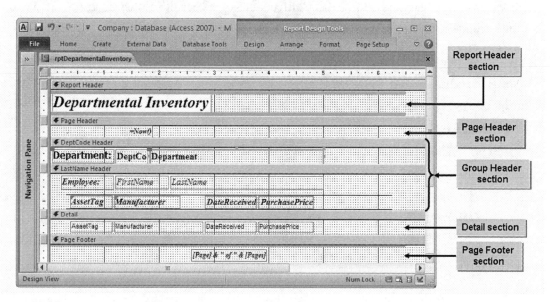

Figure 6-3: *Sections in a report.*

Commonly Used Report Controls

Access provides many commonly used controls that you can add to a report.

Control	*Description*
Text Box	Used to display values retrieved from tables and queries.
Label	Used to display headings and descriptive text.

Control	Description
Hyperlink	Used to display links to websites.
Combo Box	Used to allow users to select a value from a list or enter a value.
List Box	Used to allow users to select from a list of values.

How to Add a Control to a Report

Procedure Reference: Add a Text Box Control to a Report

To add a text box control to a report:

1. Display the desired report in the Design view.
2. On the **Design** contextual tab, in the **Controls** group, select the **Text Box** control.
3. In the document window, click in the section where you want to add the control.

Procedure Reference: Add a Label to a Report

To add a label to a report:

1. Display the desired report in the Design view.
2. On the **Design** contextual tab, in the **Controls** group, select the **Label** control.
3. In the report, click and drag at the desired location to add the label control to the report.

Procedure Reference: Rename a Label in a Report

To rename a label in a report:

1. In the Design view of a report, select a label control.
2. Rename the label.
    1. Select the existing label and type the desired label name or;
    2. Use the **Property Sheet** pane to rename a label.
        1. Display the **Property Sheet** pane.
        2. On the **All** tab, select the **Caption** property and type the desired label name.

Procedure Reference: Display a Calculated Value in a Report

To display a calculated value in a report:

1. Display a report in the Design view.
2. Select the text box control in which you want to display a calculated value.
3. Display the **Property Sheet** pane.
    - On the Ribbon, on the **Design** contextual tab, in the **Tools** group, click **Property Sheet** or;
    - Right-click the inserted control and choose **Properties.**
4. In the **Property Sheet** pane, on the **Data** or **All** tab, click the **Control Source** property and click the **Build** button.
5. In the **Expression Builder** dialog box, build the desired expression by adding the desired operators and field names.

6. Click **OK** to close the **Expression Builder** dialog box.

7. If necessary, close the **Property Sheet** pane.

8. If necessary, in the document window, remove the default label control or rename the label.

9. Save the report, and if necessary, close the database.

ACTIVITY 6-2
Adding a Calculated Field to a Report

Before You Begin:
The OGC Retail.accdb file is open.

Scenario:
As the accounts manager of your company, you created a report based on computer purchase information. You want to amortize the cost of computers over three years and include the result in the report.

1. Insert a text box in the report.

   a. In the Navigation Pane, on the rptInventory report, right-click and select **Design View.**

   b. Scroll to the right.

   c. On the **Design** contextual tab, in the **Controls** group, click the **Text Box** button.
   ![ab]

   d. In the report window, on the **Detail** section band, on the horizontal ruler, click at the 10.5-inch mark to add a new text box.

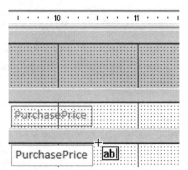

2. Display the **Expression Builder** dialog box.

   a. On the **Design** contextual tab, in the **Tools** group, click **Property Sheet** to open the **Property Sheet** pane.

   b. In the **Property Sheet** pane, on the **All** tab, to the right of the **Control Source** property, click in the blank field and then click the **Build** button. [...]

3. Add a custom calculation to the selected control.

   a. In the **Expression Builder** dialog box, in the **Expression Elements** list box, select **Operators.**

   b. In the **Expression Values** list box, double-click the equal sign **(=)** to add it to the **Expression** text box.

c. In the **Expression Elements** list box, select **rptInventory.**

d. In the **Expression Categories** list box, scroll down and double-click **PurchasePrice** to add it to the **Expression** text box.

e. In the **Expression Elements** list box, select **Operators.**

f. In the **Expression Values** list box, double-click the division sign **(/)** to add it to the **Expression** text box.

g. Type *3* and click **OK** to add **=[PurchasePrice] / 3** as the expression to the control and to close the **Expression Builder** dialog box.

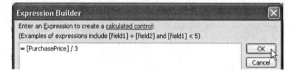

---

4. Insert a label for the calculated field.

a. In the **Property Sheet** pane, click the **Close** button to close the **Property Sheet** pane.

b. In the report document, in the **Detail** section, click the default label control for the inserted control, and press **Delete.**

 The number displayed in the label control may vary if you have deleted other controls and reinserted them when performing the activity steps.

c. On the **Design** contextual tab, in the **Controls** group, click the **Label** button.

d. Just below the **Page Header** section band, to the right of the **PurchasePrice** label, click at the 10.5-inch mark on the horizontal ruler and drag to just above the **Detail** section band to the 11.5-inch mark on the horizontal ruler.

e. In the label control, type *Amortized*

f. Switch to the Design view.

g. Scroll to the right.

h.   Observe that the report displays the Amortized column with the calculated values.

Amortized

333

433.333333333

400

400

416.666666667

5. Save the report.

a.   Select the **File** tab and choose **Save Object As.**

b.   In the **Save As** dialog box, in the **Save 'rptInventory' to** text box, type *rptMyInventory* and click **OK.**

c.   Select the **File** tab.

TOPIC C

Format the Controls in a Report

You added a control to show calculated values in a report. However, at times, you might be required to change the way data is displayed in a control based on user requirements. In this topic, you will format the controls in a report.

Assume that you are preparing a financial report for your organization. You can generate a comprehensive report by formatting the controls in the report. However, you may want to tweak the way data is displayed in certain sections, such as the annual turnover and profit and loss sections, of the report to catch users' attention. This is easily accomplished by formatting controls to display data as desired.

Control Properties

You can access the properties of a control by using the **Property Sheet** pane, which categorizes the properties into different tabs: **Format, Data, Event, Other** and **All.** The **Format** tab contains properties that define the format in which data is displayed. The *Control Source* property allows you to set or edit the data source of a control in a report.

How to Format the Controls in a Report

Procedure Reference: Format the Controls in a Report

To format the controls in a report:

1. If necessary, in the Navigation Pane, from the drop-down list, select **Reports** to display the list of reports in the database.
2. Display the desired report in the Design view.
3. In the document window, select the desired control.
4. Display the **Property Sheet** pane.
   - On the **Design** contextual tab, in the **Tools** group, click **Property Sheet** or;
   - Right-click the selected control and choose **Properties.**
5. In the **Property Sheet** pane, select the **Format** contextual tab.
6. On the **Format** tab, set the values for desired properties.
7. Set other property settings on other tabs as desired.
8. Save the report.
9. If necessary, close the database.

ACTIVITY 6-3
Formatting the Controls in a Report

Before You Begin:

The OGC Retail.accdb file is open.

Scenario:

You created a business report using Access. While reviewing the report, you think that the data contained in a particular field can be more easily understood if it is formatted appropriately. Also, you want to change the format of the date, thereby making your report appear more professional.

---

1. Change the format of the control containing the amortization expression.

    a. In the report, observe that the values under the Amortized column are displayed in general number format and in some cases lengthy decimals.

    b. Switch to the Design view.

    c. In the report window, scroll to the right, and in the **Detail** section, select the text box control containing the **=[PurchasePrice]/3** expression.

    d. On the **Design** contextual tab, in the **Tools** group, click **Property Sheet.**

    e. In the **Property Sheet** pane, on the **All** tab, select the **Format** property.

    f. Click the **Format** drop-down arrow, and from the displayed list, select **Currency.**

    g. In the **Property Sheet** pane, click the **Close** button.

    h. Switch to the Report view.

    i. Scroll to the right.

j. Observe that the values in the Amortized column are displayed in the currency format with two decimals.

Amortized

$333.00
$433.33
$400.00
$400.00
$416.67

2. Change the format of the control displaying the date to short date.

a. Scroll to the left.

b. In the **Header** section, to the right of the text "tblInventory," observe that the date is displayed in a lengthy form with the name of the month being displayed.

Thursday, December 02, 2010

c. Switch to the Design view, and in the **Report Header** section, select the **Date** text box control.

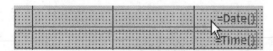

d. In the **Property Sheet** pane, on the **All** tab, verify **Long Date** is displayed in the **Format** property.

e. Click the **Format** drop-down arrow, and from the displayed list, select **Short Date.**

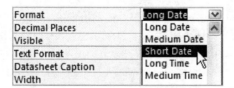

f. Close the **Property Sheet** pane.

g. Switch to the Report view.

h. In the report, in the **Header** section, observe that the date is displayed in short form.

i. Save and close the report.

TOPIC D
Enhance the Appearance of a Report

You formatted the controls in a report. At times, you may be required to change the appearance of an existing report without re-creating the entire report. In this topic, you will enhance the appearance of a report.

Imagine that you have created a report that is to be used by several departments in the organization. You now want to create the same report using a different style for a marketing presentation. Creating the report again from scratch will consume a lot of time. Access provides various features that allow you to change the appearance of a report with minimal effort.

Galleries

A *gallery* is a repository for elements that belong to the same category. It acts as a central location for accessing the various styles and appearance settings that you can apply to an object. Galleries provide you with a set of visual choices to enhance the look and feel of database elements while working on a database. For example, you can use the **Themes** gallery for accessing themes to apply to a report. Some galleries are also accessible from shortcut menus, giving you quick access to gallery options. Elements in a gallery are arranged either as a grid or in a menu-like layout.

Figure 6-4: Different controls displayed in the Controls gallery.

Themes

Access allows you to apply professionally designed *themes* to enhance the appearance of forms and reports. Several predefined themes can be accessed from the **Design** contextual tab of the Ribbon. When you click the **Themes** drop-down arrow on the **Design** contextual tab, you will see a gallery of thumbnail images representing the themes available. You can either select a predefined theme or create a theme by customizing an existing theme. Applying a theme affects all the content in a form or report by providing a consistent look and feel across all its elements.

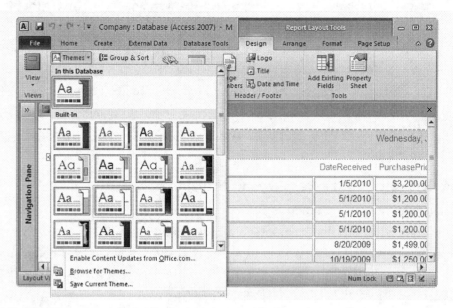

Figure 6-5: *The Themes gallery displaying themes that can be applied to a report.*

Live Preview

Live Preview enables you to preview the results of applying design and formatting changes to an element or a control, without actually applying them. These changes are displayed in the document as soon as you move the mouse pointer over the available options in a gallery. This feature provides you with a visual reference of the appearance of an object before changing a property.

How to Enhance the Appearance of a Report

Procedure Reference: Apply a Theme to a Report

To apply a theme to a report:

1. Display the desired report in the Design or Layout view.
2. On the **Design** contextual tab, in the **Themes** group, click the **Themes** drop-down arrow.
3. If necessary, in the displayed gallery, hover the mouse pointer over each theme to check the live preview of the theme.
4. Click the theme you want to apply to the report.

Procedure Reference: Add an Image to a Report

To add an image to a report:

1. Open the report to which you want to add an image in the Design view.
2. Add an image to the report.
   - Add an image in a section of the report.
     a. Select a section in the report where you want to add an image.
     b. On the **Design** contextual tab, in the **Controls** group, click the **Insert Image** drop-down arrow.
       - From the displayed gallery, select an image.

- From the displayed gallery, select **Browse,** and in the **Insert Picture** dialog box, select an image and click **OK.**

- Add an image as a control.

    a. On the **Design** contextual tab, in the **Controls** group, click **Image.**

    b. In the report, click where you want to place the image control.

    c. In the **Insert Picture** dialog box, select the required image and click **OK.**

    d. If necessary, display the **Property Sheet** pane and set the desired properties for the image control.

Procedure Reference: Add a Background Image to a Report

To add a background image to a report:

1. Open the report to which you want to add a background image in the Layout view.

2. Select the **Format** contextual tab, and in the **Background** group, click **Background Image** and select an image.

    - From the displayed gallery, select an image or;

    - From the displayed gallery, select **Browse,** and in the **Insert Picture** dialog box, select an image and click **OK.**

ACTIVITY 6-4

Applying a Theme to a Report

Data Files:

C:\084306Data\Generating Reports\Logos\Company_logo.png, C:\084306Data\Generating Reports\Logos\Company_watermark.png

Before You Begin:

The OGC Retail.accdb file is open.

Scenario:

You created a report to provide information about computers purchased for the previous month. You are not pleased with the format of the report. You could attempt to adjust a number of properties and controls, but you realize that you do not have enough time to try that out. So, you decide to use the quickest method to change the format of the report. Also, you want to add your company's logo and a background image to the reports.

---

1.   Apply a theme to the report.

    a.   Open the rptInventory report in the Layout view.

    b.   On the **Design** contextual tab, in the **Themes** group, click the **Themes** drop-down arrow.

    c.   Observe that the **Themes** gallery displays a collection of themes, which can be applied to the report.

    d.   In the **Themes** gallery, in the **Built-In** section, place the mouse pointer over the **Clarity** theme, which is the second theme in the third row. Observe that the report is displayed with a preview of the **Clarity** theme applied to it.

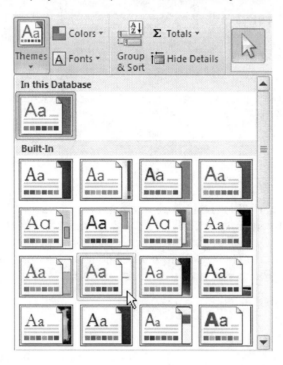

    e.   Click the **Clarity** theme.

    f.   Observe that the **Clarity** theme is applied to the report.

2.   Change the font type for the applied theme.

    a.   On the **Design** contextual tab, in the **Themes** group, click the **Fonts** drop-down arrow.

    b.   From the displayed gallery, in the **Built-In** section, select **Adjacency.**

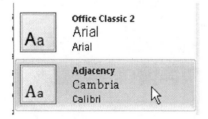

3.   Change the report title color for the applied theme.

    a.   On the **Design** contextual tab, in the **Themes** group, click the **Colors** drop-down arrow.

    b.   From the displayed gallery, in the **Built-In** section, select **Couture.**

    c.   Save and close the report.

4.   Add an image to the report.

a. Open the rptPurchase report in the Design view.

b. Scroll to the right.

c. On the **Design** contextual tab, in the **Controls** group, from the **Insert Image** drop-down list, select **Browse.**

d. In the **Insert Picture** dialog box, verify that the C:\084306Data\Generating Reports folder is selected, select the **OGC Retail.png** logo, and click **OK.**

e. In the Design view, just below the **Report Header** section band, click at the 6-inch mark on the horizontal ruler.

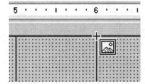

f. Switch to the Report view.

g. Observe that the company logo is displayed in the report.

h. Save and close the report.

---

5. Change the background for the rptMyInventory report.

a. Open the rptMyInventory report in the Layout view.

b. On the **Design** contextual tab, in the **Tools** group, click **Property Sheet.**

c. Select the **Format** contextual tab, and in the **Selection** group, click the **Object** drop-down arrow, and from the displayed list, select **ReportHeader.**

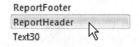

d. In the **Property Sheet** pane, for the **Back Color** property, click the **Build** button.

e. From the displayed gallery, in the **Theme Colors** section, select **White, Background 1,** which is the first color in the first row.

f. On the **Format** contextual tab, in the **Selection** group, from the **Object** drop-down list, select **Detail** to select the records displayed in the report.

g. In the **Property Sheet** pane, for the **Alternate Back Color** property, from the drop-down list, select **No Color.**

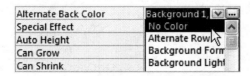

h. Click above the **Report Header** section to deselect the **Detail** section.

i. Click in the first row of the AssetTag column to select the column.

j. To the left and above the AssetTag column, click the cross-hair arrow.

k. Scroll to the right.

l. Press **Ctrl** and click the **Amortized** label control.

m. Click the Amortized column.

n. In the **Property Sheet** pane, for the **Back Style** field, from the drop-down list, select **Transparent.**

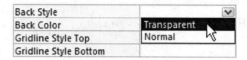

o. Close the **Property Sheet** pane.

p. Switch to the Report view.

q. Observe that the entire report is displayed with white as the background color.

6. Reduce the report display area and add a background image to the rptMyInventory report.

a. Switch to the Layout view.

b. Select the **Format** contextual tab, and in the **Background** group, from the **Background Image** drop-down list, select **Browse.**

c. In the **Insert Picture** dialog box, navigate to the C:\084306Data\Generating Reports folder, select **OGC Retail Watermark.png,** and click **OK.**

d. Display the **Property Sheet** pane.

e. Click in the first row of the AssetTag column to select the entire column.

f. On the **All** tab, for the **Border Style** property, from the drop-down list, select **Transparent.**

g. Similarly, click in the first rows of the Department, DeptCode, Manufacturer, DateReceived, PurchasePrice, and Amortized columns and set the **Border Style** property to **Transparent.**

h. Close the **Property Sheet** pane.

i. Switch to the Report view.

j. Observe that the selected image is displayed as the background image for the report.

k. Save and close the report.

TOPIC E

Prepare a Report for Print

You enhanced the appearance of reports. When improving the appearance of a report, you may notice that it contains so much information that the width of the report exceeds the size of the display area. In this topic, you will modify the margin settings to prepare a report for printing.

Though you may share electronic copies of a report, you frequently need to print them for meetings. With printed reports or other documents, you may encounter issues such as the data overflowing the page margins or blank pages being printed. It is important that you define the page setup options before printing your report to overcome these issues.

Page Setup Options

The **Page Setup** contextual tab has a collection of options that can be used to customize page properties before printing a report.

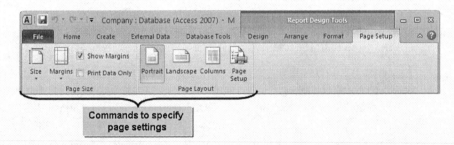

Figure 6-6: Options on the Page Setup contextual tab.

Option	Allows You To
Size	Select the size of the paper.
Margins	Set the margins of the paper before printing. It offers you three options to choose from: **Normal, Wide,** and **Narrow.**
Show Margins	View the margins in the document window.
Print Data Only	Print data without column headers.
Portrait	Print a report with the orientation set to have the height greater than the width.
Landscape	Print a report with the orientation set to have the width greater than the height.
Columns	Divide the entire page into two or more columns. After outputting data for the entire length of a page in the first column, the next set of data is output in the second column of the same page, instead of on a new page.
Page Setup	Open the **Page Setup** dialog box.

The Print Preview Tab

The groups on the **Print Preview** tab provide you with options that enable you to preview a report before printing it.

Figure 6-7: Options on the Print Preview tab.

Group	Contains
Print	The **Print** button. You can click this button to initiate the printing process.
Page Size	Options for choosing the size of the paper, setting the page margins, and printing only the data without the column headers.
Page Layout	Options for changing the orientation, adjusting the column settings, and displaying the **Page Setup** dialog box.
Zoom	Options to select the percentage of magnification at which the print preview can be viewed.
Data	Options to export a report to the PDF, XPS, text, Word document, or Excel spreadsheet format.
Close Preview	The **Close Preview** button. You can click this button to return to the view that you were using prior to choosing the Print Preview view.

How to Prepare a Report for Print

Procedure Reference: Preview a Report

To preview a report:

1. Display the desired report in the Print Preview view.

2. On the **Print Preview** tab, in the **Zoom** group, specify the preview options to preview the report.

    - Click **One Page** to view one page at a time.

    - Click **Two Pages** to view two pages at a time.

    - Click **More Pages** and select an option.

        - Select **Four Pages** to view four pages at a time.

        - Select **Eight Pages** to view eight pages at a time.

        - Select **Twelve Pages** to view 12 pages at a time.

3. On the **Print Preview** tab, in the **Close Preview** group, click **Close Print Preview** to exit the Print Preview view.

Procedure Reference: Change the Page Settings of a Report

To change the page settings of a report:

1. Display the desired report in the Print Preview view.

2. Display the **Page Setup** dialog box.

    *   On the **Print Preview** tab, in the **Page Layout** group, click **Page Setup** or;

    *   On the **Print Preview** tab, in the **Page Layout** group, click the **Page Layout** dialog box launcher or;

    *   Right-click anywhere in the document window and choose **Page Setup.**

3. In the **Page Setup** dialog box, on the **Print Options** tab, in the **Margins (inches)** section, change the margin settings of the report.

    *   In the **Top** text box, type the desired value to adjust the top margin.

    *   In the **Bottom** text box, type the desired value to adjust the bottom margin.

    *   In the **Left** text box, type the desired value to adjust the left margin.

    *   In the **Right** text box, type the desired value to adjust the right margin.

4. In the **Page Layout** group, set the page orientation.

    *   Select **Portrait** to set the height of the page more than its width.

    *   Select **Landscape** to set the width of the page more than its height.

5. Set the page size.

    a. On the **Print Preview** tab, in the **Page Size** group, click **Size.**

    b. From the displayed list, select an option to set the desired page size.

6. Click **OK** to apply the changes.

7. Save the report.

8. If necessary, close the database.

ACTIVITY 6-5
Preparing a Report for Print

Before You Begin:
The OGC Retail.accdb file is open.

Scenario:
You created a business report and are ready to print it. Because you expect a perfect output, you decide to check and alter the page settings of the report before generating a paper copy of it.

1. Preview the report.

   a. Open the rptInventory report in the Print Preview view.

   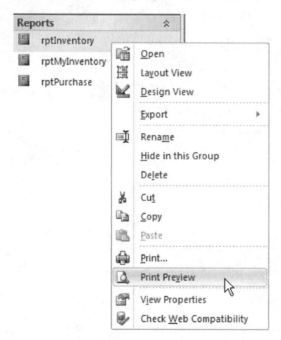

   b. Observe that the **Print Preview** tab is displayed on the Ribbon.

   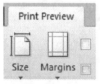

   c. On the Record Navigation bar, click the **Next Page** button.

   d. In the document window, observe that the second page of the report displays a part of the **Detail** section.

   e. Switch to the Design view and scroll to the right.

f. Place the mouse pointer over the right edge of the report and when the mouse pointer changes to a resizing pointer, click and drag the edge to the 10.5-inch mark on the horizontal ruler to reduce the report size.

2. Set the page layout for the report.

a. Switch to the Print Preview view.

b. On the **Print Preview** tab, in the **Page Layout** group, click **Landscape.**

c. In the **Page Layout** group, click **Page Setup.**

d. In the **Page Setup** dialog box, verify that the **Print Options** tab is selected.

e. On the **Print Options** tab, in the **Margins (inches)** section, in the **Left** text box, double-click and type *0.166* and press **Tab.**

f. In the **Right** text box, type *0.166* and click **OK** to apply the changes.

g. On the Record Navigation bar, click the **Next Page** button.

h. Observe that the entire **Detail** section is displayed on the first page and is not spread to the second page.

i. Close the Print Preview view.

j. Save the report.

k. Close the report and database.

l. On the **File** tab, choose **Exit** to close the Access application.

Lesson 6 Follow-up

In this lesson, you generated reports using the various report creation tools. You will now be able to produce custom reports based on specific needs for analyzing data effectively and making better decisions.

1. **Which report view do you think you will use often during the course of your work? Why?**

2. **Which report based feature in Access do you think is the most useful? Why?**

Follow-up

In this course, you examined the basic database concepts and accomplished various tasks by using the basic features and components of Access 2010. In addition, you created and modified databases, tables, queries, forms, and reports. With this knowledge, you will be able to effectively maintain and manage large amounts of information.

1. **How do you think you can improve the appearance of forms in Access 2010?**

2. **What changes to the Access 2010 user interface do you think will help you work more effectively ?**

3. **How can relational databases help you manage large amounts of data?**

What's Next?

Microsoft® Office Access® 2010: Level 2 is the next course in this series.

A | Microsoft Office Access 2010 Exam 77–885

Selected Element K courseware addresses Microsoft Office Specialist certification skills for Microsoft Office 2010. The following table indicates where Access 2010 skills are covered. For example, 3-A indicates the lesson and topic number applicable to that skill, and 3-1 indicates the lesson and activity number.

Objective Domain	Level	Topic	Activity
1. Managing the Access Environment			
1.1 Create and manage a database.			
1.1.1 Use Save Object As	1	3–B	
1.1.2 Use Open	1	2–B	2–2
1.1.3 Use Save and Publish	3	5–B	5–2
1.1.4 Use Compact & Repair Database	3	5–B	5–2
1.1.5 Use Encrypt with Password commands	3	5–B	5–2
1.1.6 Create a database from a template	1	2–A	2–1
1.1.7 Set Access options	1	4–A	
1.2 Configure the Navigation Pane.			
1.2.1 Rename objects	1	2–C	2–3
1.2.2 Delete objects	1	2–C	2–3
1.2.3 Set Navigation options	1	2–C	
1.3 Apply Application Parts.			
1.3.1 Use Blank Forms	1	5–A	
1.3.2 Use Quick Start	1	5–A	
1.3.3 Use user templates	1	2–A	2–1
2. Building Tables			
2.1 Create tables.			
2.1.1 Create tables in Design View	1	2–B	2–2
2.2 Create and modify fields.			
2.2.1 Insert a field	1	2–B	
2.2.2 Delete a field	1	2–B	
2.2.3 Rename a field	1	2–B	
2.2.4 Hide or Unhide fields	1	3–B	

Objective Domain	Level	Topic	Activity
2.2.5 Freeze or Unfreeze fields	1	3–B	
2.2.6 Modify data types	1	2–B	
2.2.7 Modify the field description	1	2–B	
2.2.8 Modify field properties	2	1–A	1–1
2.3 Sort and filter records.			
2.3.1 Use Find	1	3–A	3–1
2.3.2 Use Sort	1	3–B	3–2
2.3.3. Use Filter commands	1	3–B	3–2
2.4 Set relationships.			
2.4.1 Define Primary Keys	1	2–B	
2.4.2 Use Primary Keys to create Relationships	1	2–D	2–4
2.4.3 Edit Relationships	1	2–D	
2.5 Import data from a single data file.			
2.5.1 Import source data into a new table	2	6–A	6–1, 6–2
2.5.2 Append records to an existing table	2	6–A	
2.5.3 Import data as a linked table	3	5–A	5–1
3. Building Forms			
3.1 Create forms.			
3.1.1 Use the Form Wizard	1	5–A	5–1
3.1.2 Create a Blank Form	1	5–A	
3.1.3 Use Form Design Tools	1	5–B	5–2
3.1.4 Create Navigation forms	2	Appendix A	
3.2 Apply Form Design options.			
3.2.1 Apply a Theme	2	4–B	
3.2.2 Add bound controls			
3.2.2.1 Text box	2	4–A	
3.2.2.2 Drop down	2	4–A	4–1
3.2.3 Format Header/Footer	1	5–B	
3.2.4 View Code	3	3–A	
3.2.5 Convert Macros to Visual Basic	3	3–A	
3.2.6 View Property Sheet	1	4–C	4–4
3.2.7 Add Existing Fields	2	4–B	4–2
3.3 Apply Form Arrange options.			
3.3.1 Use the Table functions			
3.3.1.1 Insert	1	5–B	
3.3.1.2 Merge	1	5–B	
3.3.1.3 Split	1	5–B	
3.3.2 Move table	1	5–B	
3.3.3 Reposition / Format controls			

Objective Domain	Level	Topic	Activity
3.3.3.1 Anchor	1	5–B	5–2
3.3.3.2 Padding	1	5–B	5–2
3.3.3.3 Margins	1	5–B	
3.4 Apply Form Format options.			
3.4.1 Reformat Font in form	1	5–B	
3.4.2 Apply background image to form	1	5–B	
3.4.3 Apply Quick Styles to controls in form	2	4–B	
3.4.4 Apply conditional formatting in form	2	4–F	4–7
4. Creating and Managing Queries			
4.1 Construct queries.			
4.1.1 Create Select query	1	4–A	4–1
4.1.2 Create Make Table query	2	3–C	3–3
4.1.3 Create Append query	2	3–C	3–3
4.1.4 Create Crosstab query	3	2–D	2–4
4.2 Manage source tables and relationships.			
4.2.1 Use the Show Table command	1	4–A	4–2
4.2.2 Use Remove Table command	1	4–D	
4.2.3 Create ad hoc relationships	2	2–A	2–1
4.3 Manipulate fields.			
4.3.1 Add field	1	4–A	4–2
4.3.2 Remove field	1	4–D	4–5
4.3.3 Rearrange fields	1	4–D	4–5
4.3.4 Use Sort and Show options	1	4–D	
4.4 Calculate totals.			
4.4.1 Use the Total row	1	4–D	4–5
4.4.2 Use Group By	1	4–D	4–5
4.5 Generate calculated fields.			
4.5.1 Perform calculations	1	4–C	4–4
4.5.2 Use the Zoom box	1	4–C	4–4
4.5.3 Use Expression Builder	1	4–C	4–4
5. Designing Reports			
5.1 Create reports.			
5.1.1 Create a Blank Report	1	6–A	
5.1.2 Use Report Design Tools	2	5–A	5–1, 5–2
5.1.3 Use the Report Wizard	1	6–A	6–1
5.2 Apply Report Design options.			
5.2.1 Apply a Theme	1	6–D	6–4
5.2.2 Add calculated controls	2	5–D	5–5
5.2.2.1 Total report records	2	5–A	5–2
5.2.2.2 Group report records	2	5–A	5–2

Objective Domain	Level	Topic	Activity
5.2.3 Add bound/unbound controls			
5.2.3.1 Text box	1	6–B	6–2
5.2.3.2 Hyperlink	2	5–A	
5.2.3.3 Drop down	2	5–A	
5.2.3.4 Graph	3	4–A	4–1
5.2.3.5 Insert page break	2	5–C	5–4
5.2.4 Header/Footer			
5.2.4.1 Insert page number	2	5–A	
5.2.4.2 Insert logo	2	5–A	
5.2.5 Reorder tab function	2	5–A	
5.3. Apply Report Arrange options.			
5.3.1 Use the Table functions			
5.3.1.1 Insert	2	5–B	
5.3.1.2 Merge	2	5–B	
5.3.1.3 Split	2	5–B	
5.3.2 Move table	2	5–B	
5.3.3 Reposition / Format records			
5.3.3.1 Padding	2	5–B	
5.3.3.2 Margins	2	5–B	
5.3.4 Align report outputs to grid	2	5–B	
5.4 Apply Report Format options.			
5.4.1 Rename label in a report	1	6–B	
5.4.2 Apply background image to report	1	6–D	6–4
5.4.3 Change shape in report	2	5–B	
5.4.4 Apply conditional formatting in report	2	5–B	5–3
5.5 Apply Report Page Setup options.			
5.5.1 Change page Size	1	6–E	
5.5.2 Change page orientation	1	6–E	
5.6 Sort and filter records for reporting.			
5.6.1 Use the Find command	2	5–A	
5.6.2 Use Sort command	2	5–A	5–2
5.6.3 Use Filter commands	2	5–A	5–2
5.6.4 Use view types	1	6–A	

Lesson Labs

Lesson labs are provided as an additional learning resource for this course. The labs may or may not be performed as part of the classroom activities. Your instructor will consider setup issues, classroom timing issues, and instructional needs to determine which labs are appropriate for you to perform, and at what point during the class. If you do not perform the labs in class, your instructor can tell you if you can perform them independently as self-study, and if there are any special setup requirements.

Lesson 1 Lab 1

Exploring the Various Elements of the Access Environment

Activity Time: 10 minutes

Data Files:

C:\084306Data\Getting Started with Access Databases\Personnel.accdb, enus_084306_01_1_ datafiles.zip

Scenario:

Your company has invested in the Microsoft Access 2010 database to manage data, and you are given the additional responsibility of building a database that will hold this data. Before you take on this important role, you want to familiarize yourself with the Access environment. You are also asked to come out with a plan to design a database. Following the database redesign process, you need to create an appropriate design plan that includes a statement of purpose, a list of appropriate tables, and fields in each table with primary and foreign key assignments.

1. Launch the Microsoft Access 2010 application.

2. Open the Personnel.accdb file from the C:\084306Data\Getting Started with Access Databases folder.

3. Identify the various tabs on the Ribbon.

4. Explore and use the Access Help feature to find information on any database functionality.

5. Open and view the tblEmployees table, explore the different contextual tabs and close it. Then run the qryEmployees query, frmEmployees form, and rptPayAndBenefits report and view the results.

6. Write an appropriate statement of purpose for the database you intend to design.

7. After looking at the available sources of data and discussing this project with various users and stakeholders, you need to include the following fields: Name, Address, City, State, Zip, WorkPhone, DateHired, Hours, PayRate, Health, ParkName, ParkFee, and DeptName. Using the field list, organize the fields into logical tables.

8. Designate fields to be used as primary and foreign keys for each table.

9. Identify the relationships between these tables.

10. Close the Personnel.accdb database.

Lesson 2 Lab 1
Building a Customer Database

Activity Time: 10 minutes

Scenario:

The number of customers you interact with is increasing day-by-day. So, you decide to create a database to store essential information, starting with the order and contact details of the customers. Also, you want to store the data in related tables so that you can pull out the necessary information according to your specific requirements.

1. Create a blank database with the name *MyCustomers.accdb.*

2. Rename the **Table1** table *tblOrders* and insert fields named *ID, ContactID, OrderDate, OrderTotal,* and *OrderCodes* in the table.

3. Set the data type for the ContactID field as **Number,** for the OrderDate field as **Date/Time,** and for the OrderTotal field as **Currency.**

4. Create a multi-valued field for the OrderCodes field with *0001, 0002, 0003, 0004,* and *0005* as values.

5. Add a record in the table with suitable values for each field.

6. Add *Orders of the Month of March* as the description to the tblOrders table.

7. Create a table and insert the *ContactID, FirstName, LastName,* and *Email* fields in the table and save it with the name *tblContacts.*

8. Create a relationship between the tblContacts and tblOrders tables, connecting the ContactID field of the tblContacts table with the ContactID field of the tblOrders table in a one-to-many relationship.

9. Save the table relationship.

Lesson 3 Lab 1
Managing Data in a Table

Activity Time: 10 minutes

Data Files:

C:\084306Data\Managing Data in a Table\Books.accdb, enus_084306_03_1_datafiles.zip

Scenario:

You are running a book bindery business. Your database includes tables that store information about each book, each order placed, each customer, and each employee. You want to keep the data in the tables updated and access the data with ease so that the ordering process stays organized.

1. Open the Books.accdb file from the C:\084306Data\Managing Data in Tables folder.

2. Display the tblEmployees table.

3. In the table, delete the record with the employee ID "0106."

4. Display the tblCustomers table.

5. Sort the table in the alphabetical order of the values in the CustomerName field.

6. Filter data in the tblOrders table to identify the number of orders placed by Sharelife Agency.

7. Create a subdatasheet for the data in the tblCustomers table to display the orders placed by each customer.

8. In the newly created subdatasheet, for the customer ID 21965, for the OrderID 6, change the quantity value to **20.**

9. Save the file as **My Books.accdb** and close the database.

Lesson 4 Lab 1

Creating and Modifying Queries

Activity Time: 10 minutes

Data Files:

C:\084306Data\Querying a Database\Bookbiz.accdb, enus_084306_04_1_datafiles.zip

Scenario:

Your database holds a lot of information. You want to extract specific information, such as what are the books sold and how much does each customer owe for each order placed, from the database. This information will help you make important business decisions.

1. Open the Bookbiz.accdb file from the C:\084306Data\Querying a Database folder.

2. Create a query using the **Simple Query Wizard** by adding the fields BookNumber, Title, and BookPrice from the Books table; and Quantity and Date from the BookOrders table.

3. In the created query, add criteria to display the records with the value **EQ-250** in the BookNumber field for orders with a quantity over 100 and save the query as *qryEQ250.*

4. Using the qryEQ250 query, retrieve records for orders placed between 4/19/2010 and 8/12/2010 and save the query as *qryOrderBetweenDates* and close it.

5. Create a query in the Design view by adding the CustomerNumber, Quantity, and BookNumber fields from the BookOrders table and the BookPrice field from the Books table and save the query as *qryBookOrder.*

6. In the qryBookOrder query, add a field that calculates the total price each customer owes for each book order and change the calculated field name to *OrderCost.*

7. In the qryBookOrder query, group records by CustomerNumber and display the sum of quantities ordered by each customer.

8. Run the query, and before closing it, save it as *qryBookCosts.*

9. Save the file as *My Bookbiz.accdb* and close the database.

Lesson 5 Lab 1
Creating Custom Forms

Activity Time: 10 minutes

Data Files:

C:\084306Data\Designing Forms\Books.accdb, enus_084306_05_1_datafiles.zip

Scenario:

As the head of a book shop, it is your duty to keep track of the order details and the customer database updated and easy to access. You need a quick way to manipulate the information present in the database. You will create a form and enhance its appearance and usability by adding a form title and by grouping and spacing the form controls.

1.   Open the Books.accdb file from the C:\084306Data\Designing Forms folder.

2.   Use the **Form** tool to create a form for the tblOrderDetails table.

3.   Save the form as *frmOrderDetails.*

4.   Create a form *frmCustomers* using the **Form Wizard** for the table tblCustomers containing the CustomerID, CustomerName, Address, City, Region, Country, PostalCode, Phone, and Fax fields in the given order.

5.   Rearrange the controls to group the CustomerID, CustomerName, Phone and Fax fields together and the Address, City, Region, Country, and PostalCode fields together.

6.   Reset the tab order to ensure logical flow across the fields.

7.   Save the file as *My Books.accdb* and close the database.

Lesson 6 Lab 1

Creating Reports Using Access

Activity Time: 10 minutes

Data Files:

C:\084306Data\Generating Reports\Personnelbiz.accdb, C:\084306Data\Generating Reports\
Company_logo.png, enus_084306_06_1_datafiles.zip

Scenario:

Your company's employee information database contains basic data about employees, compensation, and departments. You want to compile some of this data into a report.

---

1. Open the Personnelbiz.accdb file from the C:\084306Data\Generating Reports folder.

---

2. Create a report using the **Report Wizard** to include the ParkingLotCode, EmpID, Hours, and PayRate fields from the tblPayAndBenefits table.

---

3. Save the report as *rptPayAndBenefits.*

---

4. Add a text box control and calculate the parking fee as a product of the Hours and PayRate fields. Name the field as *TotalParkingRate.*

---

5. Change the format of the PayRate control to **Currency.**

---

6. Apply a theme to enhance the rptPayAndBenefits report.

---

7. Add the Company_logo.png image to the **Report Header** section of the rptPayAndBenefits report.

---

8. Save and close the report.

---

9. Close the database.

Solutions

Activity 1-3

1. **Which is true about a statement of purpose?**

   ✓ a) The statement of purpose should not attempt to list specific table names.

   b) The statement of purpose should not imply the kinds of data that will be included in the database.

   c) The statement of purpose should not describe the likely types of database users.

   d) The statement of purpose should not include a statement of what the database will not do.

2. **In relational database design, what is the task that is performed after the review of existing data is completed?**

   a) Organize fields into tables

   b) Designate primary and foreign keys

   c) Identify the purpose of the database

   ✓ d) Make a preliminary list of fields

3. **True or False? Existing data can be available in a paper or an electronic format.**

   ✓ True

   ___ False

4. **Which statement about primary keys is false?**

   ✓ a) The primary key field can be left blank.

   b) The primary key is used to identify each record.

   c) The primary key is a field that contains a unique value.

   d) The primary key is used to establish an appropriate relationship between tables.

5. **Which statements about a field are true?**

   ✓ a) A field is a column of data.

   b) A field is not known as an attribute.

   ✓ c) There can be more than one field in a table.

   ✓ d) A field is identified by a unique field name.

Glossary

Access Help feature
A feature that provides you with a quick and easy way to find answers to Access-related queries.

Access Help toolbar
A toolbar that provides buttons which enable you to use the Help feature effectively.

Access Help window
A window that consists of components that you will require to find answers to any of the Access-related questions.

anchoring tool
A tool that enables you to position and resize the controls in a form.

AND
A logical operator that returns a true value only if two conditions that are compared are true.

arithmetic operators
The symbols that are used to perform mathematical operations.

Backstage view
An interface that appears when you select the File tab.

business rules
A company's policies and procedures that are translated into constraints that affect the input of data in a database.

calculated field
A field in which the values stored are calculated from the values stored in other fields.

comparison operators
The operators that are used to compare two or more values.

composite key
A combination of two or more fields that uniquely identifies a record.

conditional operators
The operators that evaluate the result of one or more conditions.

contextual tabs
A set of tabs with specialized commands that are displayed on the Ribbon when you select an object such as a table, form, or report.

Control Source
A property that enables you to set the source property for a new control.

control
An object used in forms and reports that helps users interact with the application.

Create tab
A tab consisting of various groups with commands for the creation of database objects.

data type
A type of data having predefined characteristics.

Database Tools tab
A tab consisting of various groups with commands for manipulating and analyzing data.

database
A collection of data that is stored logically for easy access through a computer program.

Datasheet view
A view that displays all the records in a table.

denormalization
A database performance optimization process that adds redundant data to tables to make queries run faster against very large tables.

Design view
A view that displays all the fields along with their data types and descriptions.

dialog box launchers
The small buttons that help you launch relevant dialog boxes with advanced setting options.

Edit Relationships
A dialog box that allows you to modify a table relationship or create new relationships.

existing data
The sample information that falls within the scope of a database.

Expression Builder
A dialog box that is used to select database objects and build formulas and calculations that are used with queries and reports.

expressions
The combinations of functions, field names, numbers, text, and operators that calculate a result.

External Data tab
A tab consisting of various groups with commands for importing and exporting data.

field
A column of data in a table.

File tab
A tab for displaying the Backstage view and options to open, save, and close a database.

filter
A feature that enables you to display certain data based on the data values in a column.

foreign key
A field that contains a value relating to a primary key field of another table.

form layout
The arrangement of controls on a form.

form
A graphical interface that is used to display and edit data in a table or query.

gallery
A library that lists a set of predefined styles.

Group By
The functions that perform calculations on a group of values.

grouped controls
The controls, two or more, that can be treated as one unit while designing a form or report.

Home tab
A tab that is used to organize and manipulate data in the database objects.

IntelliSense
A feature that allows you to build expressions by displaying the components of an expression when you type an expression.

join line
A line indicating the relationship between data in tables.

Live Preview
A feature that displays the result of applying design and formatting changes to an object in real time, without actually applying them.

Microsoft Access 2010
A database application that is used for storing and managing data.

Navigation Pane
A pane that is located at the left of the Access window used to access database objects such as tables, queries, forms, and reports.

normalization
A database design process that helps you produce simple table structures free of data redundancy.

NOT
A logical operator that reverses the result of a condition.

one-to-many relationship
A relationship between two tables where the primary key of one table has multiple occurrences in the foreign key table.

one-to-one relationship
A relationship between two tables where exactly one record in the first table corresponds to exactly one record in the related table.

OR
A logical operator that combines the output of two conditions and returns a true value when either of the conditions is true.

primary key
A field that contains unique values, which are used to identify records in a table.

Property Sheet
A pane that allows you to set properties for Access objects.

query criterion
A search condition that is used in a query to retrieve or manipulate specific information.

Query Design
A feature that is used to design a query in the Design view.

query
A request sent to the database to retrieve information from the database.

Quick Access toolbar
A toolbar that provides easy access to core commands such as Save, Undo, and Redo.

Record Navigation bar
A bar that is used to navigate through recordsets.

referential integrity
Validity of data in a database is enforced by ensuring that every foreign key has a link to a primary key.

relational databases
The databases that store information in multiple tables from which you can extract, reorganize, or display information.

relationship report
A feature that helps you view and print table relationships.

Relationships window
A window that displays tables in a database and the relationships between tables.

Report Wizard
A wizard that enables you to create a report by choosing fields from more than one table or query.

report
An output of data that is retrieved from tables or queries and presented in a desired format.

Ribbon
A panel at the top portion of the Access application window that contains commands under various tabs and groups.

Run command
An option that allows you to run a query from the Design view.

ScreenTip
A label mentioning the name and description of a command when the mouse pointer is hovered over the command on the Ribbon.

Simple Query Wizard
A wizard that helps you create queries by using a series of predefined steps.

sorting
A method of arranging data to view it in a specific order.

statement of purpose
A statement that helps to guide the design of a database.

status bar

A bar that is located at the bottom of the application window, which allows you to change the view of the current database object, and that displays information about the status of the application.

subdatasheet

A datasheet that is displayed within another datasheet and contains data related to the record under which it is nested in the first datasheet.

tab order

The order in which focus moves to controls within a form when Tab is pressed.

tabbed document window

A window that displays open database objects, such as tables, queries, and forms, as tabs.

Table Properties

A dialog box that allows you to add comments about a table and displays additional details such as the date on which the table was created and last modified.

table relationships

The associations that exist between one or more tables in a database design.

table

A collection of data arranged as a grid in rows and columns.

themes

The collection of colors, fonts, and effects that you can apply to a form or report.

title bar

A bar in the application window that displays the name of the database that is currently open.

Totals command

A command that enables you to add a Total row to a table that can be used to perform calculations on field values in the table.

WYSIWYG

(What You See Is What You Get) An interface that enables you to modify the layouts that you are working on.

Zoom

A dialog box that enables you to type and view the entire expression.

Index

Access Help, 8
Relationships, 61
tabbed document, 3
wizards

Lookup, 45
Report, 153
Simple Query, 94
WYSIWYG, 136